Getting Started

Getting Started: An Introduction to Dynamic Psychotherapy

Joel Kotin, M.D.

JASON ARONSON INC.
Northvale, New Jersey
London

The author gratefully acknowledges permission to reprint excerpts from "Symptomatology and Management of Acute Grief," by Erich Lindemann in *American Journal of Psychiatry,* vol. 101, pp. 141–148. Copyright © 1944 by the American Psychiatric Association.

Production Editor: Judith D. Cohen

This book was set in 11-point Garamond by TechType of Upper Saddle River, New Jersey, and printed and bound by Haddon Craftsmen of Scranton, Pennsylvania.

Library of Congress Cataloging-in-Publication Data

Kotin, Joel.
    Getting started : an introduction to dynamic psychotherapy / by Joel Kotin.
        p.   cm.
    Includes bibliographical references and index.
    ISBN 1-56821-451-0
    1. Psychodynamic psychotherapy.   I. Title.
    [DNLM: 1. Psychoanalytic Therapy—methods.   WM 460.6 K88g   1995]
    RC489.P72K68   1995
    616.89'14—dc20
    DNLM/DLC
    for Library of Congress   94-45157

Manufactured in the United States of America. Jason Aronson Inc. offers books and cassettes. For information and catalog write to Jason Aronson Inc., 230 Livingston Street, Northvale, New Jersey 07647.

CONTENTS

PREFACE

.

This book is written for therapists to read early in their training. Its first purpose is to provide information about one approach to working with patients. A beginning therapist might use the strategies I suggest, or modify them to fit his or her personality.

A second purpose of this book is to stimulate thought. The ideas in this book can be discussed with teachers and supervisors. I have tried to give the reasons for the approaches I recommend.

No one will agree with all of the views I have expressed. Differences among clinicians are useful if discussed openly. I believe it is valuable for students to recognize legitimate controversies in the field. Outstanding therapists can be found in all schools and all disciplines. Only dogmatists believe that there is only one way to work with patients in depth.

One difficulty in writing a book for beginning therapists stems from the interrelation of theory and technique. To some extent, a clinician needs to know theory before studying technique, and needs clinical experience to help make sense of theory. Some knowledge of psychopathology, and perhaps development, is required as background to understanding theory or technique. Thus it is hard to find a place to start. Nevertheless, I have attempted to write an introductory book on psychotherapeutic technique that can be read on its own.

I take responsibility for all of the views expressed in this book. I have drawn clinical examples from my own experiences as a therapist, supervisor, and teacher, and from the experiences of colleagues. In some cases I have made up composites of several real situations, and in all cases I have disguised the identities of the people involved.

I have alternated using the female pronoun for the therapist in successive chapters. Frequently I have used the opposite gender pronoun for the patient, depending on the specific examples. In all cases, no sexism is intended. Throughout the book the content applies to both sexes equally.

I am grateful to my teachers and supervisors, some of whom stand out in my memory, and others whom I know helped me, but whose specific contributions I can no longer recall. Among others, I would like to thank David Kantor, Werner Mendel, Jay B. Cohn, Frank Klein, Joe Yamamoto, Lee B. Gold, H. Arnold Meyersburg, Norman B. Atkins, Heiman van Dam, Joshua Hoffs, Morton Shane, Walter Fesuk, Justin Call, and Erving Polster.

Among those who specifically helped in the preparation of the manuscript, I would like to thank Charles Taylor and Richard P. Fox. Ilana Kotin prepared the graphics. Numerous psychiatric residents and psychology and social work interns read and critiqued the manuscript at various stages and provided invaluable feedback from those readers for whom this book is intended.

R. James Perkins patiently read the entire manuscript and gave me the benefit of his wisdom and extensive experience. Lyda Hill not only edited several versions of each chapter, but added many useful examples. Without her input, the book would be less clear, more dull, and have many more theoretical errors. I am very grateful.

Finally, I want to thank my family for their love and encouragement.

CHAPTER 1

Introduction

- Trust yourself
- The importance of "being with"
- *Understanding* is the essence of psychoanalysis and psychoanalytically oriented psychotherapy

"Trust Yourself" was the title of the first chapter of *Baby and Child Care* by Dr. Benjamin Spock—a book that guided an entire generation of nervous first-time parents. Just as new mothers need to be reassured that they have within them the natural ability to nurture their infants, first-time therapists also need to know that they have within them the potential to help a troubled stranger by the "talking treatment" that is psychotherapy.

Nothing can quite describe the anxiety of a beginning therapist with his or her first patient.[1] Whether one is a psychologist, social worker, psychiatrist, nurse, or pastoral counselor, one's career as a therapist begins with meeting just one other person, behind closed doors, with the only essentials being two chairs and a box of Kleenex.

---

[1]Throughout this book, the term *patient* will be used instead of the equally acceptable *client* (or the more unusual *customer*). Each of these terms has subtly different advantages and disadvantages.

Besides the patient and the therapist, no one else may ever know what happens in a psychotherapeutic hour. This is one of the factors that makes the therapeutic situation so fascinating, mysterious, and even dangerous (I do not only mean the rare possibility of physical danger). This privacy, which is by and large endorsed and protected by society, adds to the anxiety of the therapist, who knows that whatever he or she does will not be corrected by an instructor looking over his or her shoulder. The therapist is truly on his or her own!

In the highly charged emotional atmosphere of the first psychotherapeutic hour, *what is the therapist supposed to do? How is he or she to proceed?* In this book, I try to answer these questions.

In Chapter 2 I discuss interviewing, which is at the heart of the therapeutic process. In Chapters 3, 4, and 5 I describe one approach to the initial interview of a new patient. This includes, in Chapter 4, an outline for exploring the patient's personal history. Chapters 6 through 8 introduce some basic theoretical concepts. The remainder of the book consists of chapters on each of the three phases of psychotherapy— beginning, middle, and end—interspersed with sections on specific technical issues. The final chapter contains suggestions for further learning.

An introductory book on psychotherapy is somewhat like an introductory book on heart surgery. The field is too vast for one book to cover. Any one approach can cover only part of the territory.

Karen Horney (1942) likened the course of psychotherapy to a patient climbing a mountain with the therapist as a guide. Although the therapist has not climbed that patient's particular mountain before, he or she has had the experience of climbing other mountains and has knowledge of climbing techniques in general. This book attempts to describe some of these techniques.

Whatever else happens in psychotherapy, it is an encounter between two people. In fact, if the goal of helpfulness is added, my requirements for the *definition* of psychotherapy are fulfilled—two people talking together to be helpful to one of them.

I believe that the success of psychotherapy is dependent on the extent to which the therapist can "be with" his or her patient emotionally. Anyone who chooses psychotherapy as a career already has some degree of emotional availability and a wish to help others. The therapist should approach each patient with the wish to *listen*, to *understand*, and to *share* in his or her experience. If a beginning therapist can keep these goals in mind, I believe he or she can be taught how to be helpful. Elvin Semrad, a renowned teacher of psychotherapy at Harvard, said, "No therapy is comfortable, because it involves dealing with pain. But there's one comfortable thought: that two people sharing pain can bear it easier than one" (Rako and Mazer 1980, p. 106).

Being with the patient emotionally is necessary, but it is not enough. Nor is common sense enough. By the time most patients arrive at a therapist's office, friends and family members have already tried to help. Common sense advice has not worked. The therapist must have more than empathy and more than common sense. In fact, it can be said that *psychoanalytic* psychotherapy begins where common sense leaves off. Therapists need training to actualize their potential to be helpful.

Throughout this book, the term *psychoanalytically oriented psychotherapy* is used somewhat interchangeably with *insight therapy*, *psychodynamic* or *dynamic psychotherapy*, and *long-term* or *depth psychotherapy*. All of these terms imply a *central principle of psychoanalytic thinking*—the existence of *unconscious mental processes*, which influence behavior outside of our awareness. Helping our patients to become aware of their unconscious is one essential feature of psychodynamic psychotherapy.

No matter how far one advances in the complex, sometimes abstruse, world of psychoanalytic theory, the basic instrument of treatment remains the same—to understand the patient. All issues of technique—for example, the timing of interpretations, when to be silent, and when to confront the patient forcefully—hinge on this point. If the therapist understands the patient, he or she will know *what* to say to be helpful and *when* it should be said.

For example, a young mother was unable to leave her 6-month-old daughter with any baby-sitter, fearing that harm would come to the child in her absence. Reassurance on the part of her husband and family did no good. From the beginning of treatment, her therapist suspected that the patient's unconscious resentment of her child and the limitations placed upon her by being a mother were significant causes of her symptoms. Unconsciously, she perceived hostile or negligent impulses in the baby-sitter instead of within herself. However, it took considerable further work with the patient for the therapist to understand why this patient needed to repress (exclude from her consciousness) all resentment of her child, and how the therapist could best help her.

Significant in the patient's history were numerous abandonments by the patient's own mother. This had resulted in the patient having strongly mixed feelings toward her mother, which were unacceptable to her and therefore repressed. Unconsciously, she feared being like her mother, as well as her own rage toward her mother and her baby. These ideas were the therapist's hypotheses. However, the therapist sensed that their discussion early in treatment would not be helpful to the patient, who only allowed herself to be conscious of a narrow range of feelings.

After only a few sessions, however, the therapist found a way to approach the issue by discussing with the patient the general plight of young mothers in our society, how they have to take care of children at the cost of interrupting their careers, and often without the help of extended families that used to be commonplace. This led to a discussion of how it was quite understandable that mothers might resent their children, while also loving them. Gradually, the patient's obsessive fears decreased, and she was able to separate more normally from her child.

However, it was only after a considerably longer time in treatment that the patient was able to experience the depths of her feelings of abandonment and rage.

Often, the patient's experience of *feeling understood and accepted by the therapist* is extremely helpful by itself. I stress this point because it is basic to psychoanalytically oriented psychotherapy at all levels of proficiency. We cannot be reminded of this often enough.

An 18-year-old female rape victim greatly feared telling a male intern in the emergency room what had happened to her. She trembled as she choked out the words describing her assault.

"It must have been so awful for you," said the young doctor. "You must have been so scared."

The girl released her rigidly held body and burst into sobs. Twenty minutes later, she felt a little better.

Although the intern was not doing formal psychotherapy, his psychological encounter with the patient was highly therapeutic.

CHAPTER 2

An Approach to Interviewing

- You find out the most by saying the least
- How should the patient be treated in the consulting room? Like a guest in your home. [Ella Freeman Sharpe 1930]

The approach outlined in this chapter applies most directly to the evaluation of a new patient. However, in modified form, it applies to every psychotherapeutic interview. A therapist always wants to know "where his patient is" and how he or she is organizing his or her world.

It is a general principle of interviewing that one finds out the most by saying the least. One reason for this is simply that if the interviewer is talking, he or she is not listening, thereby losing the opportunity to gather information.

A second, and more powerful, reason for the interviewer to listen instead of talk is that *people talk about what bothers them*. If the therapist does not interfere, the patient will reveal everything significant about himself or herself.

This concept, that people talk about what bothers them, warrants elaboration. Perhaps it is easier to understand if we say that people talk about what *concerns* them. After all, how can a person *not* talk about whatever he or she is thinking about—unless there is a deliberate avoidance, as there often is in social situations, for example, by talking about the weather. Especially at first, many psychotherapy patients will try to conceal what bothers them—out of fear, shame, or guilt. For example, patients may openly discuss symptoms such as insomnia or anxiety, but may not bring up alcohol abuse or impotence for a considerable number of months. However, it is surprising how much most patients will spontaneously reveal to an interested, nonjudgmental therapist.

When a patient delays revealing sensitive information, he or she may be waiting to trust the therapist. From the beginning, patients continually "test" their therapists, scrutinizing them carefully for signs of judgment, impatience, or "hidden agendas." In *The Psychoanalytic Process*, Weiss and Sampson (1986) describe an approach in which this concept is central.

Nowhere is the principle of the therapist listening rather than talking more useful than at the beginning of the hour. The first thing a patient says is often tremendously revealing to an astute clinician, provided the therapist has not already limited the patient's freedom to express himself or herself.

HOW TO BEGIN

There are many good ways to begin a psychotherapy interview. First, the therapist should invite the patient cordially into the office. Without being frosty, the therapist should keep small talk to a minimum. The therapist may then show the patient where to sit, or let the patient choose a chair. When both patient and therapist are seated, the therapist may simply gesture openhandedly for the patient to speak, and then wait. Or the therapist may say: "Tell me about yourself," and then wait. Other good opening lines for the therapist are: "So . . ." or, "You can start anywhere you like."

All of these beginnings have the advantage of leaving the response from the patient open-ended. Thus the patient has the freest possible field in which to express himself or herself. Therapist openings such as, "What brings you to see a therapist?" or "How can I help you?" narrow the patient's freedom, thereby limiting the information available to the therapist from the patient's opening.

Furthermore, when asked for symptoms, the patient may infer that pathology is what primarily interests the therapist and will speak accordingly, sometimes even to the point of inventing symptoms to gain the therapist's approval. The therapist asking, "How can I help you?" implies that the patient should know how to answer this. He or she may have no idea how to respond, and therefore may feel more inadequate than he or she already did.

Examples

The following are examples of what can be learned at the start of an hour. Naturally, these conclusions are tentative, only serving as guides to further understanding of the patient. (Obtaining this further understanding and discussing it with the patient are major parts of the therapeutic work itself.)

Following a neutral but inviting opening by the therapist such as, "Tell me about yourself," the patient might say the following:

Patient: Well, there's not much to tell.

Such a patient is almost certainly *depressed*. The therapist might then say;

Therapist: How do you mean?

or

T: Tell me what there is.

or

>   T: It looks like you are feeling sort of down.

This last might be said only if the therapist senses this feeling from the patient. All of these responses leave the patient free to organize his or her thinking and presentation of self (if he or she can)—a therapeutic experience in itself for the patient.

Another patient might respond this way to the therapist's opening:

>   P: What do you want me to say?

This patient could be *hysterical*, asking how can he or she please the therapist. Or the patient could be *passive aggressive*, asking, "How can I please?" but not really meaning it. Finally, the patient could be a *schizophrenic* asking for structure, which he or she is unable to provide for him- or herself. The therapist could find out more by continuing,

>   T: You can start anywhere you like.

or

>   T: What would you like me to know about you?

or simply

>   T: Whatever . . .

in a friendly and nonpressuring tone.

Another category of patient openings is exemplified by:

>   P: This is a very nice office.
>   T: Thank you.

The therapist acknowledges the social compliment and then waits. The patient may simply be trying to feel less anxious in a strange situation by making small talk, or may be trying to ingratiate himself or herself with the therapist to forestall feared criticism or rejection. If the patient were to continue in this vein, such as,

> P: Where did you get that lamp?

the therapist might answer truthfully in a friendly way, and then wait again. The patient might well find this disconcerting, and if the tension in the room continued to rise, either the therapist or the patient might comment on it.

> T: Perhaps this is a difficult experience for you.
>
> P: Yes, it is.
>
> T: You said on the telephone that Dr. Jones suggested you come to see me. I'm interested in anything you can tell me.

Sometimes a patient will be so anxious in the interview situation that it is helpful if the therapist begins by mentioning it right away, such as,

> T: You seem to be pretty tense.

Even here, when the therapist has spoken first, the therapist is still following the opening of the patient—in this case, by responding to a nonverbal communication. If the patient does not respond, the therapist could add,

> T: Perhaps it's difficult to meet with a strange doctor.

Further silence might lead the therapist to ask,

T: Have you ever been in this situation before?

This still follows the patient's lead, but the therapist is now asking for the patient's associations to his or her present state of anxiety. If the patient says no, the therapist can say,

T: Well, this must be a new experience for you.

By now most patients will volunteer *something*. If the patient has had therapy before, a discussion of that experience may follow. The relation of that experience to the present situation could then be explored (see Chapter 4). Techniques for interviewing a more disturbed patient are described in Chapter 3.

Many patients will open by immediately identifying a specific problem, for example:

P: I'm having trouble getting along with my girlfriend.

If the patient does not spontaneously continue, the therapist might ask the patient for more information about what he or she has already brought up.

T: Tell me more about that.

or

T: What kind of trouble?

If necessary, while still following the lead of the patient, the therapist could ask any of the following:

T: Your girlfriend, tell me about her.

or

T: How did you meet her?

or

    T: What sort of serious relationships have you had before?

or

    T: What happened with them?

Further questions the therapist could ask include:

    T: What do you think is causing the problems you are having?

or

    T: How have you tried to deal with the problem so far?

Even the question,

    T: What examples of relationships have you been exposed to in your life?

is directly related to the patient's expressed concern and follows naturally from it, yet it also may bring up the important issue of the patient's family of origin.

Another patient's response to the neutral but inviting opening stance of the therapist might be:

    P: I've been feeling more and more depressed lately.
    T: Tell me more about that.

or

    T: Depressed about what?
    P: I don't know what.
    T: What's the depression like?

or

    T: What sort of things have been going on in your life lately?

Here the therapist can be responding empathically to the patient's mood, while at the same time waiting for the patient to furnish more information about the specific concerns of his or her life.

Other Advantages of this Technique

There are many advantages of following the opening of the patient, even to the point of trying not to introduce a subject before the patient has brought it up. For example, the first• other person mentioned by the patient in the interview is probably the most important person in the patient's life (even if the patient is not fully aware of it, for example, an ex-spouse with whom the patient is fighting in court).

The longer it takes for the patient to mention *any* other • person probably reflects how isolated (schizoid) the patient is. If a major topic or person is not mentioned (such as a spouse, handicapped child, or dying parent), it indicates at least some complexity of feeling about the situation, perhaps resentment, shame, or denial. Most of all, however, following the patient's lead enables the interviewer to *be with* the patient in his or her experience, while at the same time learning most efficiently about the patient's world.

This information-gathering and attempting-to-understand stance of the therapist is quite different from ordinary social conversation. At times the therapist may appear distant to a• patient who is looking to the therapist for approval or directive social cues. This issue relates to a fundamental tension inherent in psychoanalytic psychotherapy, between the therapist's natural social behavior and his or her behavior as a therapist.

The therapist aims to strike a balance between saying little and thereby gathering the most information, versus making the patient feel comfortable without leading the conversation in a more superficial direction. The effect of the therapist's seemingly strange behavior is ordinarily lessened, however, as the patient senses the therapist's interest and empathy. Furthermore, as the therapist learns to relax in his or her role, it feels more natural.

So far I may have given the impression that the interviewer should either be silent or pepper the patient with questions. Both silence and questioning can be overdone. Silence is further discussed below. Questioning can be a valuable tool for the therapist, especially if performed in a nondemanding, open-ended fashion. However, in many successful interviews, the patient will spontaneously do a great deal of the talking. Often there need be only a few prompts or leading questions from the therapist.

If there is a long silence, patients will frequently continue if asked. For example:

> T: Go on.

Or the therapist can simply repeat the patient's last word expectantly.

> P: Whenever my husband and I discuss money, it always leads to an argument. (Pause.)
> T: An argument?
> P: Yes, he keeps running up the debt on our charge cards without paying any attention to where we are going to get the money to pay them off.

In a typical interview, one subject frequently leads to another.

> T: Oh, your father? What's he like?

or

> T: You mentioned work. How are things going there?
> What exactly do you do? ·
> How do you get along with your boss?
> What is your income?

This last question might be too intrusive for some patients; on the other hand, the therapist's calm and sincere inquiry might help to lower social barriers.

Generally the therapist should avoid asking questions that can be answered yes or no, in favor of those that are more open-ended, for example, "What sort of serious relationships have you had before?" is preferable to, "Have you had any serious relationships before?" Questions that begin with "Why" should also be avoided, in that the patient may feel a need for self-justification: "What do you think is causing the problems you are having?" is preferable to, "Why do you think you are having these problems?"

As a teaching device in an interviewing course for psychiatric residents, I have conducted demonstration interviews with new patients, in which I *only* discussed with the patient material spontaneously brought up by him or her. Almost always, a complete history and more than sufficient material upon which to make a diagnosis emerged.

Sigmund Freud (1905a) emphasized the importance of listening and observing when he wrote, "He that has eyes to see and ears to hear may convince himself that no mortal can keep a secret. If his lips are silent, he chatters with his finger-tips; betrayal oozes out of him at every pore" (p. 78).

This approach to interviewing, that is, allowing the patient to present himself or herself and how he or she structures his or her world can be thought of as the • "Rorschach response." In describing what he sees in a neutral ink blot, a patient not only projects his inner world of emotions (for example, are the images he sees frightening or friendly?), he also reveals *how* he approaches the world. For example, an obsessive-compulsive man who sees the world as a sum of details, who "misses the forest for the trees," will focus on small features around the edges of the ink blot. A hysterical woman, who is "swept up by the swoosh of experience" and sees only the forest, will react the same way to the ink blot, taking in the whole figure with one generalization.

The patient will respond to the interviewer as he or she does to the world, and the sensitive interviewer will therefore be able to infer much information very quickly. Put another way, each of us has a *modus operandi*, an "M.O.," that is characteristic of how we deal with the world. A patient cannot help but use his or her typical M.O. with the therapist.

In group therapy, this principle is called the *social microcosm* (Yalom 1975). Each member of a therapy group will relate to the group as he or she does to others elsewhere in life. A shy person will be shy, a woman who can relate comfortably only with other women will not relate well to the men in the group. A "people pleaser" will be liked by the group (at least at first), and so forth.

In individual psychotherapy, a similar phenomenon occurs in the patient with respect to the therapist. We are discussing it here to illustrate interviewing principles. We will return to this topic in Chapters 6 and 11.

IMPLICATIONS

There are further implications of this powerful principle that one finds out the most by saying the least. It is well known that schizophrenia is characterized by loose associations. The stream of a schizophrenic's talk does not follow logical connections. If the interviewer is silent and does not provide structure for the patient (in the form of focused questions or social cues, for example) the schizophrenic patient will become "loose." Silence on the part of the interviewer is therefore, in effect, a provocative test for schizophrenia. If a schizophrenic patient does become increasingly disorganized in an interview, the therapist can try to provide structure by asking questions that can yield specific answers or by discussing concrete matters. For example:

T: Tell me about yourself.

P: Well . . . well . . . well . . . I was waiting for the bus and the bus was late . . . but then the driver . . . the driver . . . drives me crazy! Ha, ha, ha! . . . Can I get a glass of water?

T: Sure. There is water in the waiting room.

(The patient leaves and returns with a cup of water.)

T: You came here on the bus?

P: Yes.

T: It sounds like you've been having some difficulty concentrating lately.

P: (relieved) Yes.

T: Are you able to work?

(The patient is silent.)

T: Whom do you live with?

P: My mother.

Another value of relative silence on the part of the therapist relates to the universal tendency of therapists, especially when inexperienced, to interrupt their patients at inopportune times. For example, just when a patient is beginning to cry about his failed marriage, a therapist may interrupt to ask about the patient's grandparents. Or when a female patient is recounting painful details of having been molested, the therapist will interrupt with a question. Without meaning to, many therapists (and at times all therapists) inadvertently act in such a way as to lighten the patient's material instead of deepening it. Most of the time this occurs because of something the therapist says rather than because he or she is silent. Thus, more often than not, if in doubt as to whether to speak, a beginning therapist should perhaps remain silent. Experienced psychotherapy supervisors nearly always report having to tell their students to talk less with their patients.

There are at least two reasons for the tendency of therapists to interrupt their patients. One is the pressure that a therapist may feel that he or she should do something rather than just listen. Beginning therapists especially are very anxious, and being active may temporarily relieve feelings of inadequacy about their new roles. A second and more profound reason is that being with a patient who is expressing painful feelings or memories evokes similar feelings in the therapist, based on his or her own painful past. This adds to the difficulty of being with someone in pain. Many therapists unwittingly change the subject with patients to avoid their own feelings of anxiety or depression.

Another fascinating aspect of the beginnings of interviews is the notion that the first four minutes contain in miniature, in compressed and subliminal form, the entire future course of a long psychotherapy (or any other relationship). This possibility is supported by theories that suggest that a considerable percentage of communication between human beings is nonverbal (and thus may take place subliminally and very quickly). Our brains take in an enormous amount of information about people unconsciously. This accounts both for "love at first sight" and the repetitious behavior of a woman who married three abusive, alcoholic husbands in a row, in spite of believing at the time that the last two were "different." The more skilled and sensitive the interviewer, the more information about the patient and the future course of the relationship may be understood.

INTUITION

To enhance their sensitivity to others, therapists need to value their intuition. Erich Fromm believed that humans, like animals, can sense a great deal about the intentions of other individuals, but that this ability is systematically trained out of people in civilized cultures. For example, a parent might say to a child, "What do you mean you don't like Uncle Ernie? You never saw him before." I recommend that ther-· apists try to train themselves to be aware of their immediate, inner reactions to people—to feelings, smells, and fantasies. In the course of interviewing a patient, if a hunch comes, try to follow it, if it is possible to do so without derailing the patient's direction. Fears among therapists of being voyeuristic are often unfounded, and the wish to pursue a particular subject is frequently based more on sensitivity to the patient than is suspected.

So far this discussion has focused mostly on the initial psychotherapy interview. However, the principle of finding out the most by saying the least applies in significant ways to all phases of psychotherapeutic work. It is standard practice for psychoanalytically oriented therapists to let their patients begin each hour, following a social greeting. Some patients find the silence of the therapist at the beginning of each hour disconcerting at first, but most come quickly to appreciate the opportunity to express themselves in an open field. Beginning this way helps the therapist begin trying to understand the patient right from the very start and to follow Freud's famous dictum, "The patient determines the subject of the hour."

Even when the therapist has something important to say to· the patient, such as to announce vacation plans, to discuss the fee, or to raise a burning question about something that occurred in a previous hour, it is still best to let the patient begin. First, this lets the patient know that his or her concerns are first in the therapist's mind. Second, the therapist can assess where the patient is psychologically by how he or she begins. Third, something overwhelming that clearly should come first may have happened since the last hour. For example, the patient's spouse may have just asked for a divorce.

Throughout this chapter I have stressed one point of view—that you find out the most by saying the least—for the purpose of teaching. In practice, *any* deviation from this principle may be warranted for the purpose of establishing a relationship with the patient. It is an art to be able to foster a relationship, while at the same time learning as much as possible. Applications of this principle will be discussed in succeeding chapters.

CHAPTER 3

The Initial
Psychotherapy Hour:
First Third

Goals:

- Establishing rapport
- Understanding the patient's problems as he or she experiences them
- Assessing the patient

This chapter and the next two describe an approach to the initial psychotherapy hour with a new patient. The hour can be divided into thirds, with different goals and techniques for each third. This approach can be used with minor modifications in any clinical setting, such as private practice, a clinic, or a hospital.

This approach need not be carried out with mathematical precision. In practice, a considerable portion of the hour may be devoted to one or another third. Significant portions may need to be carried out in future hours. However, keeping this scheme in mind will help the therapist to orient himself or herself and the patient to the task at hand.

The goals for the first third of the initial psychotherapy hour are listed above. The first goal, *rapport*, is essential, so that the collaboration that is psychotherapy can continue to develop. However, at the beginning, rapport may only mean some sense of friendliness, as opposed to overt hostility, along with the patient's sense of the therapist as an interested person with an intent to be helpful. If the therapy goes well, however, this initial sense of rapport will develop into a sympathetic, intersubjective relationship.

Sometimes the second goal, *understanding the patient's problems as he or she sees them*, and the third goal, *assessing the patient*, coincide. An example is a man experiencing an immobilizing depression following being laid off from his job. The therapist's assessment of the problem is likely to be very similar to the patient's. Each recognizes that the patient is depressed, that this condition was precipitated by the loss of the job, and that feeling and functioning better are the goals of treatment. This is in contrast to a paranoid patient who believes he is being persecuted by signals from a radio station. He may not see a need for psychiatric treatment at all, whereas the therapist's assessment will be that the man is psychotic. Throughout the entire course of therapy, the therapist needs continually to assess the patient's current psychological functioning, because this can change. For example, some patients become more anxious, depressed, or even psychotic during the course of their treatment.

With regard to the last two goals, the therapist's ability to do two things at once, (1) to understand the patient—to *be with* him or her—while at the same time (2) to maintain a relatively objective view of the patient and the therapy, is a major source of the therapist's power to help the patient. From the beginning, the therapist must continually guard against veering too much toward one or another of these tasks.

BEFORE THE FIRST MEETING

The psychotherapeutic relationship between the patient and the therapist begins with the first contact. In private practice, this is usually by telephone—the patient calls for an appointment. I recommend that the therapist discuss as little as possible on the telephone. He or she should simply try to set up an appointment with the patient in as efficient a manner as possible. The reason for this approach is that little can be accomplished by telephone. It is difficult for the therapist to assess the effect of his or her statements, and it may not be possible to correct misunderstandings.

Talking on the phone with the patient himself or herself is preferable to planning the appointment through a third party, such as a spouse. This begins the relationship in a straightforward manner, between therapist and patient, as early as possible. The result is that the patient is less likely to feel he or she is being manipulated. If the patient agrees to come to the appointment, experience has shown that rarely will he or she object to discussing personally the arrangements, directions to the therapist's office, and so on, on the phone. (The situation is obviously different with children or early adolescents.)

If the patient feels more comfortable coming to the office with someone, the therapist need have no objection. It is preferable that the patient enter the office alone, but if he or she feels a need to bring another person, then it is probably better to proceed in that way.

Some patients will insist on the therapist answering questions on the phone, such as about fees, therapist qualifications, and so on. If the patient refuses a suggestion that it is better to talk about these things in person, the therapist has little choice but to answer. Of course, it is possible to refuse to answer, such as, "I don't discuss fees on the telephone." "Let's get together and talk," is nearly always the best solution, however.

One reason for not discussing fees on the telephone is that the therapist may want to adjust the fee after getting to know the patient. Second, in a face-to-face meeting, important, related issues may come up. For example, because of low self-esteem, a patient may feel that he or she is not *worth* spending much money on himself or herself. If a fee were simply quoted on the telephone, such a patient might give up on therapy, whereas in person the issue might be fruitfully addressed.

THE FIRST MEETING

In clinics, patients often make their appointments with a secretary or clerk, and meet the therapist for the first time at the first appointment, sometimes after an intake interview. In these situations, it is important for the therapist to introduce himself or herself and, once in private, to identify his or her role: "As I said in the waiting room, I'm Michael Johnson, and I'm your therapist here at the clinic. Tell me about yourself."

Patients in hospitals meeting their therapists for the first time especially need structure: "I'm Michael Johnson. I'm a social worker here at the hospital, and I'm going to be your therapist while you're here. We'll be meeting three times a week, and I'll see you every weekday in group therapy. (Pause) Tell me about yourself."

If the therapist has the option of arranging his or her own office furniture, there are a few time-honored traditions. First, there should not be a table or a desk between the patient and therapist. This encourages direct communication. Second, the therapist and patient should have similar chairs. This encourages a sense of equality and self-esteem in the patient. Third, many therapists feel that the patient and therapist should sit near enough so that they could touch if one or the other reached out. This encourages intimacy. Finally, I recommend allowing the patient to choose where he or she sits. The therapist might say, for example, "I'm Michael Johnson. Come in. Sit anywhere you're comfortable."

If one chair is identified as the patient's chair, it should be nearest the door. This enables a frightened patient to have the feeling he or she can leave. In a hospital, if a patient is either menacing or visibly frightened, I recommend not only placing the patient nearest the door, but even leaving the door ajar. The therapist could say, "I'm Michael Johnson, and I'm going to be your therapist while you're here. Come on in and sit down. I'm going to leave the door open a little, and if you get uncomfortable, you can leave at any time." Placing the therapist between the patient and the door runs the risk of making the patient feel cornered, and therefore more likely to feel frightened and become assaultive. If the therapist feels too afraid of a particular patient, he or she should not meet with that patient alone.

In private practice, the therapist can introduce himself or herself to the patient in the waiting room, and then invite the patient into the office. Once they are seated, and after sometimes unavoidable small talk (which may, however, help to relax and engage the patient), the therapist can say, "Tell me about yourself."

GOALS OF THE FIRST THIRD

Although all three goals of the first third of the initial hour are important throughout the therapy, *understanding the patient's perceived problems* occupies a special place in the beginning of the first hour, first because it addresses a primary concern of the patient, and second, because discussing it will enhance rapport and permit further assessment of the patient. The patient will sense that the therapist is on his or her side, interested in what is important to him or her.

As mentioned above, the patient's perception of his or her problem may not necessarily be the same as the diagnosis.

For example, a patient may complain primarily of obsessive thoughts or insomnia, while meeting all the *DSM-IV* criteria for major depression. Patients with so-called character dis-◦ orders are said not to perceive their difficulties as stemming from within, and often approach treatment reluctantly, at the instigation of others. These patients are best approached in the same manner: starting with what the patient perceives or realizes. For example, the therapist could say, "So your wife says you have a drinking problem. What makes her think that?"

The interviewing techniques described in the previous chapter constitute one powerful approach to understanding the patient's perceived problem. I have heard experienced therapists say that for the first part of the hour, the patient gets to free associate about *anything*. This doesn't necessarily mean free association in the psychoanalytic sense (described in Chapter 6), but only that the therapist should listen to whatever subject the patient wishes to discuss.

Understanding the patient's perceived problem is often accomplished with little difficulty. For example, a patient (Mr. A.) felt depressed following rejection by his girlfriend. He reported being able to think of nothing else:

> T: Tell me about yourself.
>
> P: I guess I'm here because two weeks ago my girlfriend and I broke up. I can't seem to get over it. I just want her back. I don't know what to do. I can't stop thinking about her. I send her flowers and letters. She won't return my calls. I can't sleep. I've never felt so miserable. I'm a nervous wreck.
>
> T: How long were you two together?
>
> P: A year and a half.
>
> T: Tell me what happened.
>
> P: She just said she needed some space and that we shouldn't see each other for while. (Pause)

> T: What did she mean by "a while"?
>
> P: She said we shouldn't see each other for three months.
>
> T: What happened?
>
> P: She said I was too possessive.
>
> T: What did she mean?
>
> P: Well, I'd get really jealous if she'd talk to another guy.

In contrast to the above situation, it may be very difficult to establish a mutually understood view of the patient's problems, as with some depersonalized or psychotic states. The patient may be silent, or not address what, at first, seems like any focus at all.

> T: Tell me about yourself.
>
> P: There is nothing anyone can do.

In this situation, the therapist can only provide structure, emphasize his or her desire to help, and try to understand.

> T: (After allowing a pause) I'm not sure what you mean. Do about what?

When a patient is in crisis, it may be necessary to spend nearly the entire first hour on a pressing problem (for example, acute grief or a sudden marital separation). Only at the end need a plan be made, which may be nothing more than an agreement to meet again, perhaps the next day, to continue the discussion.

A longer "first third" may also be necessary when the patient's speech is obsessively detailed, circumstantial, or vague.

On the other hand, if the patient is very anxious, or sensitive about a particular subject, it may be better to go on to the agenda of the middle third of the hour at the beginning (postponing the assessment, etc.). Later the therapist can return to the patient's problem after he or she has had some time to settle down and become accustomed to the interview situation.

If the patient *is* able to discuss his or her problem, considerable material about the patient's life and history will emerge in the discussion. For example, in the case of Mr. A., described above, the therapist could ask for more details about the patient's possessiveness, about past relationships, about his friends' responses, about his parents as models of relationships, and about his job as a source of strength or a further burden during this stressful time.

Hearing how the patient thinks his problem developed, and what he himself has done to try to deal with his difficulties, gives important indications of his adaptive capacities (ego strength). For example, Mr. A. tried to woo his girlfriend back by sending letters and flowers. That having failed, he could not see much of a life for himself without her, even a long time into the future. He was reluctant to look very deeply at his own contributions to difficulties in the relationship. Each of these aspects could be explored further, either later in the initial hour or in subsequent hours.

A description of the problem from the patient's point of view is sometimes called the patient's *chief complaint*. The next step is then called the *history of the present illness*. These categories simply constitute a relabeling of this goal of the first third of the initial psychotherapy hour.

DIAGNOSIS

Assessment of the patient is a goal in the initial and all subsequent psychotherapy hours. This does not necessarily mean a formal diagnosis according to *DSM-IV*. (Contrary to appearances, psychiatric diagnosis does not enjoy a unitary consensus within the field. For years a formal debate was held at the annual scientific meeting of the American Psychiatric Association about the value of the *DSM* diagnostic category approach.) It is much more important for the purposes of psychotherapy to have a general idea of how well put together the patient is, and to have an idea of the patient's personality style—his or her usual modes of functioning.

I have found it useful to follow Otto Kernberg loosely (1984) in dividing patients into three broad categories: neurotic, borderline, and psychotic. This can be done according to the degree of primitiveness of their defenses, capacity for mature object relations (that is, relationships with people), and ability to perceive reality accurately.

The nature of the patient's difficulties will reflect his or her ability to test reality and to relate to others in a mature way. For example, Mr. A. did not seem to manifest a serious disturbance of reality testing, but his single-minded attachment to his girlfriend suggested some problems with object relationships, perhaps an unusually high degree of dependency. Mr. A.'s level of defenses is less apparent from the small sample of the interview presented above, but the nature of his presentation suggests an all-or-nothing, black-and-white view of the world (either he is with his girlfriend or he is devastated). This is consistent with some degree of splitting, a relatively primitive defense. Furthermore, he felt jealous when his girlfriend spoke with other men, reflecting his own insecurity and, perhaps, a paranoid trend.

Thus, Mr. A. might initially be presumed to have a high or middle level borderline personality organization. This impression would have to be continually monitored by the therapist, who might revise upward or downward the assessment as the therapy proceeded. Paraphrasing Greenson (1967), it is sometimes possible to arrive at a reliable psychodynamic diagnosis only after a long period of psychotherapy.

In practice, some psychotherapy patients will be in the

neurotic range, while many will have some degree of borderline personality organization, which can be thought of as
high, middle, or low.

The ability to recognize severe borderline personality
disorders and psychosis is acquired gradually. Chaotic histo-
ries and bizarre symptoms are suggestive of severe problems,
but they are not conclusive. Disturbances of association are
more diagnostic, but these are sometimes rather subtle.
Nearly everyone has had the experience of listening to
someone talk, seeming to follow the connections, only to
realize after a while that the entire discussion does not make
sense. This may be an example of loose associations and
suggestive of psychosis.

These few, rather broad categories of diagnostic impression are useful to a therapist in the sense of what to expect
from the patient, and therefore what treatment strategies to
use. Generally, the more disturbed the patient, the less the
therapist can expect in terms of rapid change. The question
of different approaches with relatively healthy or highly
disturbed patients will be discussed more in Chapters 6 and
8. However, an old adage highlights the limitations of psychiatric diagnosis: "Each patient is his own textbook."
Semrad expanded this idea by saying, "Therapy is therapy—
talking to the patient about what matters to him, no matter at
what pace he can take it" (Rako and Mazer 1980, p. 102)

ORGANICITY

A *mental status examination* is sometimes recommended as
part of a psychotherapeutic evaluation. In practice, it is
rarely necessary to follow rigorously the categories of a
formal mental status examination. However, if organic im-
pairment is suspected, it is then more important to perform
at least an abbreviated mental status examination. Although

the complete examination is beyond the scope of this book, if the patient is (1) alert, (2) oriented to time, place, and person, and (3) has no defect of *recent* memory, significant organic dysfunction is highly unlikely.

Level of consciousness (alertness) and orientation will generally be deducible from the patient's material. If it is necessary to test recent memory, I generally ask the patient's cooperation in a memory test. If he or she agrees, I ask him or her to repeat a simple sentence, such as, "Tom and Bill went fishing and caught three bass." After a few minutes of discussion of other matters, I ask the patient again to repeat the sentence. This is a simple but surprisingly subtle test. If a patient has *any* difficulty repeating the sentence verbatim, such as forgetting the names of the men or the number of bass, then a more careful assessment for organicity is in order.

CONCLUSION

After the first third of an initial psychotherapy hour, the therapist would like to have *some idea of the patient's problems as the patient sees them*. The therapist may also have some *initial diagnostic ideas* about the patient's level of functioning, but these might be very tentative.

Once again, after twenty minutes with the patient, the therapist may not have any clear ideas about what is going on. If so, this is data for the therapist, and could indicate a difficult or obscure clinical situation. It could also be a reflection of the therapist's inexperience. Even if this is the case, however, the therapist should not become discouraged. The correct path is simply to continue to try to understand the patient. Sooner or later this approach will bear fruit, and the therapist and patient can continue to develop their ability to work together.

A patient with some knowledge of psychology demanded to know the theoretical orientation of his therapist. "What approach do you feel would be best for you?" replied the therapist. This led to a discussion of what the patient felt he needed, and his ideas of the cause of his symptoms.

An even more demanding patient, a large, impressively dressed man, immediately challenged his therapist. "What are your credentials? Why would you be a good therapist for me?" Needless to say, the therapist felt on the spot. However, she did not react defensively and list her credentials, nor was she angry or too passive. Instead, she said, "I don't know, we'll have to see. The question is, how can we learn to work together." The patient relaxed and a helpful collaboration eventually developed.

Considerably more understanding about the patient's life can be gathered as the therapist proceeds to the second third of the initial hour, when specific data are added through taking a history.

CHAPTER 4

The Initial Psychotherapy Hour: Middle Third— Taking a History with the Mnemonic Device "FEW MAPS"

- Family
- Education
- Work

- Medical
- Alcohol (and other drugs)
- Prior psychotherapy
- Sexual

Some psychotherapists take a history from their patients and some do not. Although I believe it is possible to practice competent psychotherapy without ever obtaining a formal history, because everything important will surface eventually, I recommend taking at least a brief history as part of the first (or at least, the first few) interviews.

Obtaining a history is best done face to face. Written questionnaires for patients detract from the personal encounter, and, especially if presented to the patient before meeting the therapist, create a mechanical impression. Furthermore, new patients may be so anxious that they leave out important facts, or they may lie.

Taking the history rounds out the picture of the patient revealed in the beginning of the initial psychotherapy hour.

The additional information helps the therapist understand the patient's dynamics and functional abilities, and helps the therapist decide on a diagnosis. Having this information as early as possible helps in the crucial area of treatment planning (a goal of the final third of the initial hour).

The therapist can commence taking the history (the middle part of the initial hour) after learning something of the patient's view of his or her problem and its background (the chief complaint and the history of the present illness). Of course, much important historical material may have emerged in the discussion so far, and the therapist may already have made some diagnostic inferences. However, the less the therapist has been able to make these inferences, the more valuable will be the information obtained in the history.

For taking a history, I recommend the mnemonic device "FEW MAPS," which stands for family, education, work, medical, alcohol (and other drugs), prior psychotherapy, and sexual. This a useful guide to what a brief but thorough psychological history should contain. FEW MAPS is also a useful reminder that when doing psychotherapy, one cannot simply follow a method or map, that ultimately each patient *is* his or her own textbook.

Frequently it is not possible to obtain all the FEW MAPS information from the patient in the first hour or even the first few hours. With experience, however, much of the information can be elicited early, and the unknown areas can be kept continually in mind.

FAMILY

The therapist seeks information about the patient's current family and his or her family of origin. With regard to *current family*: Is the patient married? For how long? How old is the spouse? What is his or her occupation? Any children? Their sex and ages? How are they doing? Prior marriages? How long? How and why ended?

If an adult has not married, and if his or her history of relationships has not been discussed thus far in the interview, the therapist could inquire now about any close relationships in the patient's life. If a personable man or woman in his or her late thirties is single, that may be as revealing as a history of three divorces. The patient's family in adult life generally reflects his or her capacity for relationships and intimacy. These data are not only the pattern in the fabric of the patient's life, they are the threads that make up the cloth.

Another example might be a man who has had no contact with his children from a prior marriage. Not only is such a man isolated from people who were once important to him, but he is also failing his children's needs for a father. On some level he is aware of this, though it may not be spoken of by the patient or the therapist for a considerable period of time. (And if the therapy is short term, it may never be spoken of.)

The therapist may or may not comment on any of the information revealed in the patient's history. The information obtained is, in a sense, supplemental to that related to the patient's primary problem. Furthermore, it is important to emphasize that *inferences or generalizations*, such as the ones in the above paragraph, are only tentative guesses that should be lightly held by the therapist and continually revised as the therapy unfolds.

Equally important, compared with the patient's current family, is his or her *family of origin*. Were the patient's parents his or her natural (birth) parents? Were they together? Was their marriage calm or stormy? If there were separations or divorces, whom did the patient stay with? What were the stepparents like? What were the parents' occupations? Who was at home to take care of the children?

What was it like growing up in that family? Who was the boss? What were the ethnic factors?

Does the patient have siblings? How many? Brothers or sisters? What was the birth order and time between their births? Such information is especially revealing, for example, with regard to the so-called middle-child syndrome.

One version of the middle-child syndrome goes as follows: When a first child is born to a couple, they usually welcome the child, regardless of its sex. This child lives in a happy paradise—he or she has both parents to himself or herself. Then the second child is born. The first child feels abandoned and resents the interloper, although the extent to which this is manifested varies considerably. Then the third child is born. The first one says to himself or herself regarding the second, "See, now what happened to me is happening to you," and allies with the third against the second. The second allies with the fourth, and so on. In big families, this alternation of sibling alliances is sometimes quite regular.

If there are only three children, the first gets to be oldest and the third gets to be the baby. The middle child may be left out. So much the worse if the first two are boys and the third is a girl, or vice versa. The closer the children are in age, the less energy the parents may have had to give, exacerbating the problem.

Sibling birth order powerfully affects character. Knowing this history helps the therapist form hypotheses. For example, a first child may grow up self-confident or with a feeling of having been betrayed or rejected. A middle child may feel depressed, unloved, or angry. The "baby" of a family may feel either indulged or neglected.

A depressed female architect in her thirties described both of her parents as alcoholics. She was the fourth child born in the family, and the fourth girl. Two years later a baby brother was born, with a hand deformity that required several operations. Not only were both parents relatively unavailable due to alcohol abuse, but the patient, yet another baby girl, was a severe disappointment to them. Her brother not only got more attention for being a boy, he also was the focus of parental attention because of his deformity. All her life the patient struggled with feelings of unworthiness and anger, until she was able to work these out in psychotherapy.

It is often useful to ask a patient, "Who were you closest to growing up?" Some patients will name a parent or a sibling, some a grandparent or a teacher; some will give the chilling response, "No one." The woman described above had been closest to her second oldest sister, with whom she still had a markedly ambivalent relationship. However, what mothering she got seemed to have come from that sibling.

Regarding the patient's family, or any other topic, anything *unusual* is interesting and revealing to the therapist. Not having children is as much an event as having eight, or having two, ten years apart. A childless couple may have decided not to have children, or perhaps there were miscarriages or medical problems, accompanied by psychological trauma. There might have been serious marital conflict, which may or may not have centered on the subject of having children.

EDUCATION

Sometimes this inquiry can be limited to a single question, "How far did you go in school?" If the patient dropped out of high school in the eleventh grade, it might have been due to pregnancy, economic necessity, wanting to get away from home, delinquency, a psychotic break, a learning disability, fear of success, or something else. College may have been interrupted for similar reasons. In each case, the therapist will ask what happened. If a highly intelligent person has little education or a low-level job, the reasons for that are certainly intriguing to the therapist.

WORK

If it has not yet come up, the therapist might ask, "How are you supported?" If the patient works, the therapist might ask for details about the job, if they have not already been provided. How long has the patient had his or her job? What is the longest job the patient has ever held? What happened at the last job(s)? For example, does the patient have a problem with authority, or with his or her own success?

Especially with relatively disturbed patients, the length of time of the longest job can be an important marker of functional capacity. Examples of a longest job might be two weeks at a fast-food restaurant, three months as a waitress, or two years as a stock clerk. Each of these probably represents a progressively higher level of mental health.

It is also important to ask about military service. This is such a significant event in a person's life that the therapist should know about it, and its effects, if possible. Was the patient's discharge honorable? If not, the reasons are important. These might include criminal behavior, psychosis, or homosexual issues.

MEDICAL

The therapist should know about any hospitalizations or serious illnesses in the patient's past. A patient who spent her sixth grade year in bed in traction for a back injury may have had an especially difficult experience of puberty. High blood pressure, colitis, or migraine headaches may be the result of how the patient deals with stress in his or her life. Diabetes or heart disease are important ongoing stressors. Such events as surgeries, abortions, or cancer chemotherapy can have important emotional aftereffects.

Does the patient currently take any medications? The answer may reveal the presence of current illnesses, or possible dependence on tranquilizers or sleeping pills. Not knowing about medical issues in a person's life can be a serious oversight by a therapist.

ALCOHOL AND OTHER DRUGS

If the patient senses a serious, nonjudgmental attitude on the part of the therapist, he or she will often frankly answer questions in this area. On some level, the patient may want help with these issues. On the other hand, patients may not reveal the extent of their substance abuse for a long time. At Boston City Hospital, we were taught to multiply by four whatever number of drinks per day a patient admitted, to get a true figure.

Once the subject has been broached without bristling, the therapist can ask specific questions, such as, "What do you drink? At what time of day? How long does a fifth last?" or, "How many packs of cigarettes do you smoke a day?" or, "How big is your habit?" (meaning, how much money per day do you spend on heroin?). If the patient perceives that he or she has a drug problem, how has he or she attempted to deal with it so far? With what results?

PRIOR PSYCHOTHERAPY OR OTHER
PSYCHIATRIC CONTACT

This is important information for many reasons. First, it may reveal how serious the patient's problems have been in the past, for example, if the patient has been hospitalized. Second, the therapist will better understand how the patient is approaching *this* therapy by knowing how past encounters went. For example, if in the past the patient was forced to go to a therapist by a parent or a court, he or she will have a different attitude now than if prior treatment had been sought voluntarily.

The outcome of prior treatment(s), if any, is very important as a *predictor* of the outcome of the current treatment. If a prior psychotherapy was progressing but then the therapist moved away, it would seem logical to predict that the patient probably can work in therapy, but will try to guard himself or herself against the therapist's abandonment.

If the patient has made three tries at psychotherapy, but has quit each one after just a few sessions, the prognosis for another therapy is likely to be poor, unless the issue of leaving therapy early is dealt with immediately. For example, the therapist can ask the patient if he or she discussed his or her dissatisfaction with the prior therapist. The therapist can ask the patient if he or she will agree to discuss negative feelings about *this* therapy as these develop. Further, "How would it feel for you to tell me that the therapy isn't helping, or that something I said hurt your feelings?"

A chronic alcoholic or schizophrenic who has been through many institutions may have an understandable skepticism about how much help he or she can expect to receive. The therapist's acknowledgment of this, and the reality of the reasons for it, will help to establish valid communication, and paradoxically, a beginning sense of trust.

SEXUAL

Patients (and sometimes therapists) often avoid discussing this important subject because of anxiety or embarrassment. Yet, frank inquiries can lead to open answers. The therapist can ask, "Did your relationship with your boyfriend include sexual intimacy?" or "How is your sex life with your wife?" If the patient responds, "Yes" or "Fine," the therapist has learned little. However, he or she can then ask, "How frequently do you have intercourse?" "Is it satisfying for both of you?" "Would either of you like to have sex more or less often?" Problems in sexual functioning are often difficult for men to talk about, and need to be approached sensitively. Masturbation fantasies are often not revealed for long periods of time. However, the careful therapist can frequently elicit important information in the early hours of therapy by asking the patient directly.

In some situations, it may not be tactful for the therapist to bring up sexual issues in the first hour. For example, if the patient is in crisis about losing his or her job, or the death of a parent, dealing with those issues will take precedence over other topics. If the FEW MAPS outline is kept in mind by the therapist, however, these other important areas will be approached when the time becomes appropriate.

FEW MAPS is useful as a general guide to history taking. All the information might not be obtained immediately, but if the therapist keeps these categories in mind, significant information is less likely to be missed.

With regard to learning the important details about our patients' lives, it has been said with tongue in cheek that psychotherapists are the *stupidest* people—they never understand anything! They are always asking, "I don't understand. Could you tell me more about that?"

CHAPTER 5

The Initial
Psychotherapy Hour:
Final Third

- Therapeutic intervention
- Recommendations
- Contract

Sometimes the best therapeutic intervention a therapist can make in the first hour is to support the patient's decision to begin psychotherapy. This support includes empathic contact, recognition of the patient's suffering, and most importantly, the communication of hope that proceeding with therapy implies.

Some therapists like to make a trial interpretation near the end of the first hour. This can serve two functions: (1) to assess the patient's capacity for insight psychotherapy, and (2) to begin to establish the way in which the patient and therapist can work together.

One example might be:

> T: You are very angry at your boss who bullies you. You have also told me that your father was very domineering. This seems to point to a theme in your life.

The therapist then waits. How the patient responds may give some indication of how open the patient is to recog-

nizing unconscious connections within himself, and, infer-
entially, how open he is to change.

Regardless of a specific therapeutic intervention, in the
final third of the initial psychotherapy hour, the patient and
therapist need to reach an agreement about how the therapy
is to proceed. As a first step the therapist needs to communicate his or her conclusions and recommendations to the
patient. Following the patient's response, the therapist and
patient can then agree on a treatment plan—an agreement or
contract. (As used here, the word *contract* does not imply a
formal, written document, nor should the word be used with
patients, but it emphasizes the purposeful and mutual nature
of the agreement between therapist and patient.)

One example might go like this:

> T: On the basis of what you've told me, I think you're
> depressed and struggling with a number of issues. I think
> that you could benefit from psychotherapy. I would sug-
> gest that we try meeting twice a week for a while and see
> how we work together.
>
> P: Well, okay.
>
> T: Ordinarily we'll meet for 45 minutes and my fee is
> one hundred and twenty dollars. (If the patient has no
> response at the moment, the therapist can continue.) I
> could see you on Tuesdays and Fridays at 9 A.M. Does that
> work for you?

Sometimes it is useful for the therapist not to try to
establish closure, but to suggest using the first few sessions as
an "extended evaluation."

> T: You've told me a lot about yourself and your prob-
> lems. I think psychotherapy might have a lot to offer you,
> and perhaps medication would also help. Why don't we
> schedule a few more meetings as a kind of an *extended
> evaluation*, and see how we both feel about it?

Sometimes it is worthwhile to separate the therapist's recommendation from the plan:

> T: I think therapy is a good idea for you and it seems like you think so too. Now the question is how to arrange it. You could see me, or I could help you find someone else. What would you like to do?

Sometimes the therapist and patient cannot work out mutually agreeable arrangements, for example, if the patient needs evening or weekend sessions and the therapist has chosen not to work those hours. Sometimes a therapist needs to help a patient find another therapist who charges a lower fee.

The subject of the fee for psychotherapy merits considerable discussion. Frieda Fromm-Reichmann remarked that psychotherapy is priceless if it succeeds and worthless if it fails. So what is a right fee? Usually it is a compromise between the going rate in the community, what the patient can afford, and what the therapist feels comfortable with.

A colleague of mine remembers his first private patient. When the patient asked him his fee, he said, "One hundred . . . (gauging the patient's reaction) and ten!"

Some therapists prefer to have the patient pay at the end of each session. I make that request only if the patient has a history of alcoholism or other drug abuse, gambling, or difficulties in handling money (compulsive spending, for example). Otherwise, I find it easier to be paid monthly, and, if the patient does not need a bill for insurance or other specific purposes, I do not make one. If I do make a bill for a patient, I hand it to him or her at the end of the month, which personalizes that part of the relationship (and saves time, envelopes, and postage). At the end of a first session, if it is not clear that the patient is going to return, I ask for payment at that time.

T: Could you write me a check for today?

Beginning therapists often feel guilty for charging the patient anything. It is important for the therapist not to set a fee so low that eventually he or she begins to feel resentful. However, it is also important to remember that the fee can nearly always be renegotiated, especially if there has been a change in the patient's financial circumstances. Sometimes it is useful to agree on a fee only for a specific period of time, for example, six months. There can be an agreement to review the fee at the end of that time.

At times it seems best not to try to make long-range plans in the first hour, either because the patient is skittish or the material is very hot.

T: I can see that you're upset about your marriage ending, and I think it's good for you to talk about it. How would it be if we meet again tomorrow to continue?

(In this conclusion, there is no mention of a fee or a contract beyond the next day. Those issues will need to be dealt with in the next session. In effect, the therapist is extending the initial session into two or more hours.)

Often it is very reassuring to the patient if the therapist *expresses directly a wish to help*.

T: I can see that you've been through a lot and have tried to cope with it. *I'd like to help you.* I think we should meet regularly to work on it. How do you feel about that?

If the patient has not had a recent medical examination, it is a good idea to recommend one.

T: I doubt that your depression (or anxiety) has a direct physical basis, but that sometimes occurs. I would recommend that you have a thorough medical examination in the near future. We can discuss the results if you like.

After the therapist makes a recommendation, or even after a tentative agreement (contract) has been reached, it is often useful to ask the patient, "Before we stop, is there anything else I should know about you?" This will sometimes yield extremely valuable information, which may have been withheld up to that point.

Assuming that the therapist feels that psychotherapy is in the patient's interest, "hooking the patient" is clearly a goal of the initial hour. Questions such as "How worried about yourself are you?" can be helpful, both to promote realistic self-evaluation by the patient and to help the patient recognize a need for help. However, it is also important that the patient be allowed as much freedom as possible to come to his or her own decision. Attempts to pressure the patient are usually counterproductive.

If a patient seems to be responding ambivalently, the therapist could say,

> T: Starting psychotherapy is an important decision. I think it's good that you've come here to explore your options. Maybe you'd like to think over what we've talked about. Why don't you call me later in the week and let me know what you've decided.

If the patient does not call for, say, a week, then the therapist can follow up by telephoning. In this situation, the patient has usually decided not to pursue therapy (at least with that therapist), but the therapist's call will help the patient bring closure to his experience, and the therapist can offer noncoercive encouragement and help.

> T: I was wondering what you decided to do about therapy.
>
> P: I've decided to wait.
>
> T: Well, if things change and you'd like to meet again,

please feel free to give me a call. I'd be pleased to see you again, but if you feel I'm not the right person for you, perhaps I could suggest some other names.

There is a great deal of variability in how an experienced therapist will conclude a first hour, but the following items • should always be considered: First, the therapist should make a *recommendation*, which might be as simple as suggesting another meeting, or could include further recommendations, such as a physical examination, an evaluation for psychotropic medication, or even formal psychoanalysis.

Ideally, this recommendation should include some of the therapist's thinking or conclusions about the patient. This could be a summary of the patient's situation, for example,

> T: It seems like there is a pattern in your relationships. After promising beginnings, none of them go very far. You're starting to look at your part in this, and I think that such an approach can be very helpful.

On the other hand, the therapist might comment only that the patient is in pain and should talk about it.

Second, there needs to be a contract or agreement be- • tween therapist and patient as to how the treatment will proceed. This should include the following:

1. Dates and times of future appointments. In the beginning, as illustrated above, these may not be set regularly or far in advance.
2. Length of sessions—45 or 50 minutes is usual.
3. Fees.
4. Estimate of duration. Most often the expected duration of therapy is unknown. Sometimes it is clear to the therapist that months or even years will most likely be required, as opposed to weeks. I believe the therapist should give some indication or his or her thinking in

this area, even if only to say that the length of treatment is unknown at present and will be determined by
mutual agreement. Sometimes it needs to be added
that, of course, the patient can leave at any time.

The explicit stating of these elements of the contract
provides structure for the patient, so that both parties know
what to expect. Some issues, such as phone calls to the
therapist, missed sessions, vacations, and so on, might not be
covered at this time, but remain to be worked out. This
entire external structure is sometimes called the *frame*,
implying that the picture *within* the frame—the content of
the patient's material and the development of the relationship between patient and therapist—can be as unfettered as
possible.

If the patient chooses not to return, the therapist can still
feel good about the encounter. He or she has done his or her
best to understand the patient, evaluate the problem(s), and
convey an honest opinion. Patients invariably respect that on
some level. The patient may return at some time in the
future. If the patient sees another therapist, he or she will be
better off for having had the experience of the first therapist's sincerity and candor.

Finally, there may be considerable benefit from a single
session, even if this is not overtly acknowledged by the
patient.

A sophisticated woman in her late thirties sought consultation with a therapist, Dr. B. Although highly successful
in her career, she had not achieved the satisfaction that she
had anticipated from her position. She described her
family life as tolerable but unexciting. She was currently in
weekly psychotherapy with another therapist, Dr. A.,
which had been ongoing for seven years.

Dr. B. concluded that the patient should consider psychoanalysis for what seemed to him to be a chronic,

characterological depression, and made this recommendation to her. (This was probably an error on the part of Dr.
B. First, there was little exploration of her current therapeutic relationship. The patient might have been better off
if Dr. B. had recommended that she try to work out her
difficulties with Dr. A. Second, the decision to undertake
such a prolonged and demanding procedure as psychoanalysis should probably be made more cautiously.)

The patient then asked what psychoanalysis consisted
of. Dr. B. explained that it meant coming to therapy four
or five times per week for several years, and doing her best
to free associate, telling her therapist all that came to her
mind.

The patient reacted immediately, exclaiming, "I've
never been that close to anyone!"

The interview ended shortly thereafter, and Dr. B.
never heard from the patient again.

It seems a reasonable inference that the patient learned
something about herself from this encounter.

A similar occurrence (of patient flight) involved a con-
struction worker who sought therapy for the first time for
insomnia. During his initial hour he began to relate how he
had been repeatedly beaten by his domineering father. He
then began to cry with shaking sobs, as he remembered the
pain and humiliation. The therapist tried to prevent his
regressing too quickly, but with minimal success. The hour
ended with the patient saying that he would "think about"
futher sessions. Only six months later did he return for a
second session. "That first time scared the shit out of me,"
he related.

To paraphrase Erik Erikson, hopefully your patient will
emerge from his encounter with you more whole and less
fragmented than he was before.

When it goes reasonably well, the initial hour will end
with some mutual agreement about future meetings. Both

the patient and therapist will have a sense of the beginning of a successful collaboration.

Later chapters describe the three phases of psychotherapy—beginning, middle, and end—in which the themes presented thus far are elaborated and worked out. Understanding the patient remains the primary therapeutic instrument, because it promotes both insight and the relationship between therapist and patient.

Before proceeding to the course of psychotherapy, however, it is necessary to describe certain introductory concepts.

CHAPTER 6

How Does Psychotherapy Work?

- Six curative factors
- What about proof?

How does psychotherapy work? This question has been asked for over one hundred years. Many explanations have been proposed. Perhaps the question, How do people change in therapy? is as difficult to answer as, How is character formed? or, Why do people do the things they do?

Five curative factors in psychotherapy are frequently described. These are:

1. Suggestion
2. Education
3. Abreaction
4. Insight
5. Identification.

We will also discuss a *sixth factor*, as yet undefined.

SUGGESTION

Suggestion means giving advice to the patient—telling him or her what to do. A therapist may give overt suggestions to a patient, for example,

>   T: At twenty-five, it's time for you to separate from your
>   parents. You need to get a job and move out of your
>   parents' house.

While this advice might be helpful in encouraging a patient
to take some important maturational steps, it can go wrong
in any number of ways. For example, the patient might take
the advice but never feel he made this important decision for
himself. Or he might try to take the advice but psychologically be unable to manage the separation and therefore
become psychotic. Or the patient might not take the advice.
Then he might feel like a failure in the eyes of his therapist or
like the therapist's disobedient child.

Sometimes the therapist's suggestion seems trivial.

>   T: I think you would benefit by getting an accountant to
>   do your taxes.

Even this advice, however useful, infantilizes the patient,
implying that the therapist knows best how the patient
should manage his affairs. To the extent that the patient believes that the therapist really does know better, the situation
worsens because the patient has devalued himself.

Sometimes the therapist's advice is essential—for example, recommending a medical evaluation to rule out organic
causes of depression.

At other times a therapist may feel strongly compelled to
give advice. This may be because of experiences in the
therapist's own life:

>   T (reflecting on his own divorce): You need to see a
>   divorce attorney right away so you don't get screwed in
>   court.

Or the therapist may be responding to a patient's painful
situation:

> T: If your husband *ever* hits you again, you should call 911. And then you should press charges against him.

Here the therapist intends both to protect and empower the patient. However, even this advice may have some of the unintended negative effects described above.

Suggestions may be covert as well as overt:

> T: You mean when your husband hits you, you don't do anything about it?

Ordinarily, *the more competent the psychotherapist, the less advice he or she gives*. Often, a therapist can find other ways than suggestion to achieve a particular goal. Here is one approach to a situation of spouse abuse:

> T: So whenever you have an argument with your husband when he's been drinking, you get hit.
>
> P: Yes, I guess so.
>
> T: Can you think of any way you could stop this from happening?
>
> P: Well, when he's like that, he won't let me leave. (Pause) I suppose I could call 911.
>
> T: When you think about doing that, something stops you?
>
> P: I guess I'm just afraid.
>
> T: Of what?
>
> P: I don't know. Standing up for myself, maybe.
>
> T: What will happen if you don't do anything differently?
>
> P: I guess it will just keep happening.
>
> T: You've told me that you think it's really bad for your kids, as well as for you.

P: It is.

T: So what are you going to do if he does it again?

P: I guess I'll call 911.

T: Could you do that?

P: (Pause) Yes.

T: What do you think would happen then?

And the therapist and patient continue to work on the issue.

Undoubtedly some suggestion occurs in every psychotherapy. For example, therapists generally imply to patients that it is good to think before acting, and to try to understand their dreams. However, this general principle applies: If suggestions are helpful, they infantilize the patient and make the therapist seem omniscient; if suggestions prove harmful, then they shouldn't have been given anyway.

Sometimes a therapist will have a hard time regarding whether or not to give advice:

A 30-year-old woman told her therapist that she had been molested from age 6 to 11 by her uncle. She had never told anyone before, and her uncle had recently died. Because the uncle was known to have had a shady past, the patient felt her parents should not have left her alone with him. She felt angry at them for not protecting her. She also loved them, and felt a strong need for them to continue to love her. She feared that if she told her parents, they would either blame her or not believe her, and would withdraw their love.

This patient repeatedly pressed her therapist to tell her what to do. Should she tell her parents? Her therapist felt pressured both by the patient and by a popular book that recommended that sexually abused children of all ages should stop "being the guilty bearers of family secrets." Furthermore, for a period of some time, the patient seemed "stuck" both in her therapy and in important areas of her life. Perhaps if she told her parents it would break the logjam.

The therapist told the patient he did not know what she should do, but pointed out that it was important that she develop within herself the *capacity* to confront her parents. Then she could choose whether or not to do so, free of internal blocks. The patient recognized within herself strong motives both to tell her parents and to keep silent. Finally she concluded that telling her parents would hurt them unnecessarily. She could not be sure that the news would not cause her father to have an immediately fatal heart attack.

The issue remained difficult for both the therapist and the patient, who later ended her therapy without having achieved many of the goals she had sought. The therapist never completely resolved within himself whether he should have supported more firmly the patient's impulse to confront her parents—an approach that seemed to him to border on suggestion.

If a helpful suggestion has been given to a patient, for example, to call 911 to deal with domestic violence, then at some future time, the therapist should acknowledge with the patient the effect of the advice and the patient's reaction to it.

T: You're sure doing better with your family since you stood up to your husband's hitting you.

P: Yes.

T: Maybe there is a wish that I could always tell you what to do in a crisis.

P: Yes, I guess there is. That would be nice.

T: So because I can't, you're facing a loss. Of course, you were able to hear what I said, and you acted on it by yourself. Maybe you won't need me so much in a future crisis.

EDUCATION

The second factor, *education*, means giving information to the patient. One focus of educational statements by the therapist may be the external world at large. Some examples:

T: You could find a good internist by calling a local medical school. If a doctor is board certified and teaches in a medical school, he or she is likely to be competent.

T: There are special schools for dyslexic children in this area.

T: You may be eligible for vocational training from the state.

T: You may be eligible for psychiatric disability.

A second focus of education by the therapist may be the patient's interpersonal world.

T: Several short telephone calls each week to your mother in the nursing home are probably more helpful to her than one long call.

T: With children, it is important to have immediate consequences for misbehavior, and also to realize that a five-minute "time out" may too long for a 3-year-old.

T: Many men don't realize that just listening to their wives' feelings is being actively helpful. Sure, she needs encouragement to look for a new job after being fired, but it is also important to listen to her pain—to be with her emotionally, without having to fix it right away. After all, if your best friend is jilted by his girlfriend, you can't do anything about it, but he needs your shoulder to cry on.

Finally, the therapist may try to educate the patient about the internal world or about how to use psychotherapy.

T: There is a difference between feelings and actions. When you say you "get angry," which do you mean? I presume you know that it is possible to feel something strongly *without* acting on it. It's an idea from pop psychology that all a person has to do is get his feelings out. After all, if an employee tells his boss off, he's probably going to get fired.

T: Your role here is to feel free to tell me everything that occurs to you, without censoring anything.

T: Even though you're quite upset with me, things seem to be going better for you in your life outside of the therapy hours. It's generally better if a person's life is going well while her therapy is stormy, than if her life is stormy while she enjoys her therapy.

As with suggestion, education is a part of all psychotherapy. The above examples illustrate the variable role that education can play in psychotherapy. For example, learning the difference between feelings and actions can be crucial for some patients.

On the other hand, direct educational statements, like suggestion, can easily be overdone. If there is too much education, the therapy becomes more like a class with the patient passively taking in information (assuming that he *does* take it in), rather than the vital encounter between two people and the work in depth that make psychoanalytic psychotherapy so uniquely powerful.

In a broad sense, all psychotherapy can be considered education, in that the patient learns about himself or herself, with guidance from the therapist.

ABREACTION

Abreaction is the expression of feelings or affect, especially those connected with the memory of a traumatic event. A strong expression of such feelings is sometimes called a *catharsis*. When Freud first started trying to cure hysteria in the late 1800s, he developed the cathartic method. At the time he believed that if his patient relived a forgotten, painful memory, along with the *full expression of her emotions* connected with the event, she would be cured. Later he realized that this alone was not enough to solve many of his patients' problems.

Nevertheless, the expression of emotion is an essential part of psychotherapy. A person may hold in his or her feelings consciously (*suppression*), or unconsciously exclude them from awareness (*repression*). The rape victim described at the end of Chapter 1 suppressed her feelings in an attempt to control what she felt to be unbearable pain. She felt better after relieving her pent-up emotions.

It is common for patients to experience previously unconscious feelings, as these become accessible during the course of therapy.

A 40-year-old assistant plant manager struggled over whether to ask his intimidating boss for a raise. To his therapist, he described his extra efforts for the company, his successes in increasing production and lowering costs. The therapist said, "It seems to me like you feel you've contributed a great deal to the company, and it doesn't sound like you've gotten much recognition."

The patient exploded: "You're damned right. All that little prig of a boss does is sit on his ass and take the credit for my work! (Pause) God, I didn't know I felt so strongly!"

This is an example of the lifting of *repression*. Repression can apply to feelings, as in this example, or to ideas or memories (Moore and Fine 1968).

Further discussions over time revealed the patient's intense anger both at his boss and his father, who had also denigrated the patient's achievements. The expression of this anger in his therapy helped the patient to see his relationships with both men more clearly. He was then able to ask his boss for a raise in a direct and appropriate manner.

• The value of catharsis is recognized in the conventional wisdom of "having a good cry," the healing power of laughter, and the usefulness of "getting it off your chest."

Significant changes that occur in psychotherapy are nearly always associated with strong expressions of affect at some point. The therapist's ability to "be with" the patient is especially important at these times.

As will be discussed in Chapter 9, the expression of genuine feelings by the patient is one of the few usually reliable signs of progress in psychotherapy.

INSIGHT

Insight has long been held to be a central mechanism of change in psychoanalytically oriented psychotherapy. Insight means understanding the unconscious meaning of one's behavior, perceptions, thoughts, and feelings.

In the above example of the intimidated assistant plant manager, the patient's attitude and behavior toward his boss were similar to how he had related to his father. Throughout his childhood, the patient had endured his father's constant sarcastic criticism. The boy's reaction had been to cower, and constantly try harder to please his father. The boy had repressed his anger. Although his father was rarely pleased, the patient continued his pattern of self-effacing hard work in other areas of his life. This gained him some successes, for example, in his schoolwork and even professionally, but left him unable to assert himself toward domineering male authority figures.

After recognizing his anger at his boss in his psychotherapy, the patient began to understand that he had felt the same way about his father. He learned to use this knowledge to help him see both men more accurately as bullies, and to relate to them more assertively.

Insight may apply to patterns of behavior developed in childhood, as in the above example. Insight may also apply to unconscious hidden agendas, as in the example of the mother who feared leaving her child (whom she unconsciously resented), described in Chapter 1. As above, a patient may gain insight into his or her *behavior*, *perceptions*, *thoughts*, or *feelings*, since each of these may be influenced by powerful unconscious factors.

Other examples of insight:

A fastidious man hated immigrants because they were "dirty." As he understood his *own wishes* to be messy and more sexual (which he equated to being dirty), his hatred decreased.

A mother who was overly strict with her adolescent daughters regarding contact with boys became more lenient as she recognized her own repressed sexual impulses.

A man who constantly feared being attacked by muggers realized the enormous amount of rapacious anger he harbored, and was then able to go outside more comfortably.

• One reason for the power of insight to bring about change is the universal human tendency to form *repetitive patterns of behavior.* When these patterns are maladaptive or self-defeating, we call them neurotic. The central problem of neurosis can be formulated as, *Why don't neurotics learn from experience?* These patterns are frequently unconscious. Nearly everyone is familiar with situations where friends or relatives do the same self-destructive thing over and over again. An example is the case of the woman who married three abusive alcoholics in a row. Consciously, she believed that the second and third men were "different."

Neurotic patterns can be considerably more subtle than this. For example, an attractive man repeatedly found that relationships with women "just didn't work out." He concluded, "There just aren't any good women available." An intelligent salesman never quite became a top producer. He complained that there was always some external reason for his mediocre performance—his boss didn't like him, it was bad economic times, he didn't get a good territory, and so on.

Even when these patterns are recognized by the patient, change may not occur. It is important to realize that insight • into one's unconscious without emotional expression (abreaction) is seldom very helpful. The assistant plant manager voiced a good deal of anger in his therapy, as he remembered how he had been put down by his father as well as by his boss. The woman who had married three alcoholic men was able to make a better relationship with a man only after considerable work, which involved remembering and expressing the horrors of her childhood. This expression of affect that accompanies effective insight is part of what is called *working through*.

The power of insight ultimately rests on the ability of human beings to use their intelligence to understand themselves and alter their behavior, given the new information developed in the course of psychotherapy. Allen Wheelis (1956) adds that insight also "implies a belief that no inner danger is so bad but that knowing about it will be better than not knowing" (p. 172).

IDENTIFICATION

The fifth curative factor is *identification* with the therapist by the patient. The therapist hopes that the patient will adopt an attitude of observing and trying to understand himself or herself, just as the therapist tries to understand the patient. The concept of identification includes such ideas as imitation, incorporation, and introjection of aspects of the therapist.

The patient becomes partly like the therapist, as the patient experiences him or her. A patient may thus acquire an increased capacity to reflect on his experience and the ability to delay gratification (especially useful for an impulsive patient). Conversely, a patient who is too isolated or intellectual may develop the ability to experience and tolerate difficult feelings.

• *Thoughtfulness* (the ability to reflect) and the *ability to tolerate difficult feelings* are especially important qualities for many patients, and are mostly learned through the process of identifying with the therapist. The therapist serves as a model in his or her work with the patient. For this reason, the therapist must "be with" the patient in a real and involved way for therapeutic change to occur. An emotionally distant therapist will not be effective.

The rape victim referred to in Chapter 1 undoubtedly sensed the real concern and empathy of the intern in the emergency room. It was as if he had said, "I can stand to hear how awful this was for you. Share your pain and lean on me for a while." This permitted her to cry.

The therapist of the intimidated plant manager knew how it felt to be bullied and shamed. The patient sensed his therapist's openness to these painful feelings, and thus felt free to reveal himself.

The function of the therapist in helping a patient deal with painful or frightening feelings is sometimes described as providing a *holding environment* (analogous to a mother holding a panicky baby) (Winnicott 1965). A similar idea is expressed in describing the therapist as a "container" for the patient and his or her painful feelings and other unwelcome experiences.

Much of the identification that takes place in psychotherapy is unconscious. Without it necessarily being imme- • diately evident, the patient absorbs both the therapeutic attitude and something of the personality of the therapist, especially the part of herself that the therapist displays at work. Of course, it is also possible that the patient will absorb negative aspects of the therapist's personality.

For the patient, psychotherapy is always two challenges: • an encounter with himself and an encounter with another person. In a very loose way these two major themes correspond to *insight* and *identification*.

Identification could also be called *attachment* or *connection*, as it relates to the emotional relationship between the therapist and the patient. Patients sense the attachment of their therapists, and this devotion to the patient is itself a helpful factor. Freud (McGuire 1974) described even psychoanalysis as "in essence a cure through love."

Implicit in all psychotherapeutic work is some sort of

belief in the patient by the therapist (Kotin 1986). In some cases, it may take the therapist some time to develop this attitude toward the patient.

A 60-year-old woman displayed a spiteful attitude toward her 42-year-old daughter. At first her therapist felt repelled by the coldness of this mother. Only after hearing the history of her extremely traumatic background, the incestuous conception of her daughter, and the daughter's antisocial behavior, did the therapist begin to sense the mother's strength and dignity. Typically, even the most destructive behaviors include attempts at integrity and dignity.

RESUMED GROWTH AND PSYCHOLOGICAL DEVELOPMENT

The five curative factors described above are present, in different proportions, in all psychotherapeutic work. However, experience has shown that the whole is more than the sum of the parts. This constitutes a sixth curative factor, which is more difficult to describe than the previous five. Intrapsychic *integration* has been proposed as a term for it. Loewald (1960) described it as the effect of a more mature psychological organization on a less mature one. Put another way, most therapists agree that successful psychotherapy enables an individual to resume blocked growth and psychological development. All therapy is about growing up.

Figure 6–1 illustrates the interrelation of these six curative factors.

As implied at the beginning of this chapter, a complete description of how psychotherapy works has yet to be written. It is likely that the future will continue to bring new developments in this area.

Figure 6–1. How Therapy Helps:
A Diagrammatic Representation of Six Curative Factors

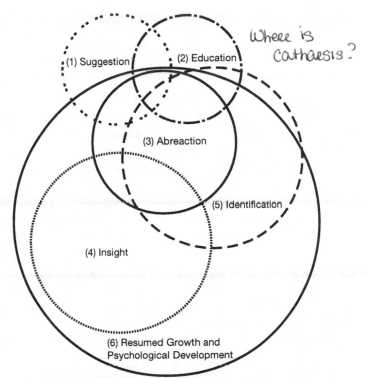

Suggestion (1) and education (2) overlap with each other. Abreaction (3) can overlap with all factors. Insight (4) is separate from suggestion and education. Identification with the therapist (5) can overlap with all factors. The circle representing the resumption of growth and previously blocked psychological development (6) includes all factors and represents the idea that the whole is greater than the sum of the parts. The growth circle does not include all of suggestion, education, or identification, because these factors can produce slavish imitation or compliance, which may not lead to growth.

(There may be exceptions to the above schematization. The diagram is only intended to convey generalities.)

WHAT ABOUT PROOF?

"Has it been proved that psychotherapy is helpful?" an aspiring therapist might ask. Many therapists worry about this issue from time to time. It is reassuring that the over-whelming majority of research studies on the outcome of psychotherapy have concluded that most patients benefit from the procedure.

Although there are a large number of psychotherapy out-come studies, it remains difficult to verify the outcome of long-term psychotherapy in the same scientific way that penicillin has been shown to cure strep throat.

One research problem is assessing changes in the patient following therapy. Asking the patient about the results of therapy may yield some useful information, but the patient could be brainwashed by the therapist, fooling himself, or even unaware of changes.

Asking the therapist for her assessment of the outcome is risky because of the therapist's self-interest.

The views of the patient's family, friends, or associates might be sought, but these may be prejudiced. For example, if the patient formerly was a "doormat" and now asserts himself, that might be seen as negative by others, when it is actually positive, or vice versa.

Elaborate batteries of psychological tests before and after therapy are cumbersome, expensive, and not universally accepted. Furthermore, whatever measurements are used to assess the patient will probably not include such subtleties as the patient developing a physical illness or having an auto-mobile accident after therapy. These seemingly unrelated events are to some extent authored by individuals and can be related to the outcome of therapy.

Control groups present additional problems. It's difficult to control all of the factors that influence psychological growth and well-being, such as prayer groups or traumatic events. Furthermore, participation in a long-term study may be undermined by factors such as geographic moves, health problems, flagging commitment to the study, and so on.

The therapist who wishes to rely on outcome studies of psychotherapy for reassurance faces further difficulties. Even if it were proven that two-thirds of all patients benefited significantly from long-term psychotherapy, what about the other one-third?

How would a therapist react if she believed that one out of every three patients that she treated, sometimes over a period of many months or years, did not benefit from the work? Even if only an occasional patient does not improve, this might be extremely difficult for a conscientious therapist, who might feel guilty or inadequate.

The director of training at a well-regarded university training program always recommended that each psychiatric resident have at least one "hopeless" case in his or her caseload. This assignment helped the therapists accept that some patients do not change. Conversely, to the surprise of everyone, a hopeless case sometimes improved.

The problem with attempting to evaluate the outcome of psychotherapy is that psychotherapy is not a standardized procedure. It is as much an art as a science. Therapists are not interchangeable, and each patient–therapist dyad is unique. How can one scientifically measure the effect of one person on another?

The best answer to a therapist's fears about the futility of therapy is the authenticity of the encounter. As Lacan (1993) put it, "Some patients will talk about themselves, but not to you. Some patients will talk to you, but not about themselves. When a patient can talk to you about himself, then his therapy is completed" (p. 161, translation modified). As long as the therapist is seriously working toward deeper engagement and is honest with himself or herself and with the patient, then I believe the patient will be affected—an impact will be made on his or her life.

CHAPTER 7

Introductory Concepts and Definitions

- Transference
- Countertransference
- Defense mechanisms
- Resistance
- Interpretation
- Psychic structure

This chapter is an introduction to some of the terms most commonly used in discussions of psychotherapy.

TRANSFERENCE

Transference is defined as the experiencing of a person or situation in the present as if it were a person or situation from the past. A person may transfer perceptions, feelings, and behavior. These reactions do not necessarily fit the present, but at one time they applied to persons or situations in the past.

Transference is a distortion, an error in time and space. Its opposite is *clarity* of perception and experience, seeing things as they actually are in present reality, without coloration from past images.

Transference is primarily unconscious. When people transfer, they believe they are seeing accurately and reacting appropriately.

The timid assistant plant manager (introduced in Chapter 6) experienced his boss in a way similar to how he had experienced his domineering father. And in relation to his boss, he experienced himself as just as powerless as he had been as a little boy. In fact, he now had many more behavioral options as an adult. For example, he could ask for a raise in an assertive manner, or he could try to speak with his boss's superior, or he could try to find another job, and so on. However, he did not see these options, and felt as trapped as he had been in his childhood. This was a *transference reaction*.

The woman who had married three successive alcoholic men had had an alcoholic father, who was usually emotionally unavailable to her as a child. However, on occasion he was very loving to his little daughter. She had learned to wait for these episodes, enduring long periods of his absence in between, and making up stories as to why her father did not attend to her. When she chose men to marry, she unconsciously equated their unavailability to that of her father, and felt attracted to them.

Transference has one additional peculiarity. Sometimes the events of the past are reexperienced in the present, not as they were but with the additional distortion of a wish fulfillment. The woman described above idealized each new man, as she wished her father had been.

This tendency of individuals to add a wish fulfillment to a transference perception partially explains erotized transferences to therapists. These can be particularly difficult clinical problems and are discussed in Chapter 11.

Transference is especially powerful when what a person cannot remember is relived in a transference, as a kind of action memory.

> A woman who had lost her mother in childhood repeatedly clung to relationships with both men and women. She would do almost anything to prevent someone from leaving her. Although she barely remembered her mother, throughout her life she acted as if the loss of any person would be unbearable.

Transference is present to some extent in all human relationships. A human being is never completely free of shadows from the past. We meet each new experience with unconscious preconceptions from the past. These transference attitudes can be global or specific.

Global transference reactions apply to all persons encountered by the individual. For example, if a child was raised by harsh and inconsistent parents, he or she is likely to expect all other human beings to behave in the same way. Such a person might become a suspicious loner—a "paranoid character." Conversely, a child raised by loving and consistent parents might develop an easygoing, sunny disposition. He or she would generally like people, and expect them to treat him or her well.

Some *specific transference reactions* were illustrated above. As another example, a woman comes to an emergency room for a minor trauma, a cut needing stitches. A male intern sews her up without complications. From then on he is a hero to her. She sends him letters and gifts and goes out of her way to see him as often as she can. As far as he knows, he did nothing in particular to deserve such attention.

Conversely, the same intern might sew up another woman's laceration, again without complications. This woman, however, has a strikingly negative reaction to him. She complains about him to the hospital administration, and tells everyone she knows to avoid him at all costs. Again the intern is mystified as to his part in this drama.

These experiences, familiar to all physicians, are examples of primitive, nearly psychotic-level transferences. These are at a nearly psychotic level because of their strength, the suddenness of their development after a relatively brief contact, and the "all good" or "all bad" role assigned to the doctor by the patient. The patient is giving evidence of relatively poor reality testing. In general, the greater the transference distortions, the more disturbed the patient.

Any reaction is never one hundred percent transference. There is usually a nidus of truth (or much more) contained in the perception. In the case of the assistant plant manager, his boss may really have been a tyrant who abused the patient. It was the patient's reaction of childlike helplessness that constituted the transference.

Transference occupies a special place in psychotherapy. Inevitably, patients form transferences to their therapists. This provides both the greatest difficulties in the treatment and the greatest opportunities for helping the patient. Freud (1912a) wrote,

> It cannot be disputed that controlling the phenomena of transference presents the psycho-analyst with the greatest difficulties. But it should not be forgotten that it is precisely they that do us the inestimable service of making the patient's hidden and forgotten erotic impulses immediate and manifest. For when all is said and done, it is impossible to destroy anyone *in absentia* or *in effigie*. [p. 108]

This last sentence refers to the emotional involvement the patient develops with the therapist (and vice versa), which makes the treatment vivid and effective.

Some transferences are present at the beginning of psychotherapy, and others develop and change as the treatment evolves. At the beginning, the therapist is frequently seen by the patient as an authority figure, similar to parents, teachers, bosses, and others. The patient frequently fears the therapist's disapproval, and also looks up to the therapist as wise and all-knowing. The therapist can frequently lessen these early transference reactions by comments such as,

> T: Perhaps you're afraid I'll judge you because of your drinking problem.

> T: There's a lot I don't understand about your patterns. Perhaps we can understand things together as we go along.

It is the fact that there is always a parental transference in the therapy situation that makes sexual (and other) exploitation by the therapist so easy and so wrong.

The transference reactions that develop over the course of therapy are often the most powerful. Transference reactions to the therapist may be positive or negative, toward mother or father, and infinite combinations and shades in between.

The assistant plant manager frequently felt his therapist was slighting, denigrating, and bullying him. The patient complained that the therapist did not understand the patient's accomplishments at work in spite of difficult obstacles. The patient felt cut off at the end of sessions, and pushed around when the therapist asked him to change the time of an appointment. In each case the patient was able to see that he was reacting to the therapist just as he had felt with his father and his boss. This understanding lessened his resentment toward his therapist, and helped him understand how pervasive were the damaging effects of decades of his father's criticism.

The woman who had married three alcoholic men soon felt she was in love with her (male) therapist. It later became clear how she experienced his therapeutic reserve and absences (the time between sessions) as similar to her father's distance. The times she felt understood by her therapist corresponded to the occasional intense attention she had received from her father. Following a period of strong negative feelings toward both her father and her therapist, she became able to appreciate and use the intermittent intimacy with her therapist, to mourn his (idealized) romantic unavailability to her, and to find a suitable marriage partner.

The term *transference neurosis* is used when the patient • has focused much of his or her energy and transference on the therapy and the therapist. It represents a new version of the patient's problems, now focused on the therapist. When this happens, the potential for change is heightened because the difficult issues in the patient's life now revolve around the therapist. When a transference neurosis develops and is resolved through understanding its origins, the greatest potential for change can be realized.

To illustrate the concept of a transference neurosis, a child therapist once described a 6-year-old boy who was phobic about dogs, frequently refusing to leave the house for fear he would meet a dog. The phobia could be understood as a displaced fear of the boy's punitive father. However, the development of the transference neurosis in therapy only occurred when the boy experienced not fear of his father, but fear of the therapist.

The working out of the patient's transference to the • *therapist constitutes a major part of the therapeutic work in insight psychotherapy.*

The transference neurosis and its resolution are idealized concepts. Frequently treatment does not proceed this way. On the one hand, a transference neurosis may not develop.

Conversely, some intense transferences turn out to be extremely difficult to resolve.

For a time it was thought that the transference could be enhanced by the therapist presenting to the patient as a blank screen so the patient could project his or her transference onto the therapist to the maximum extent. An analyst was supposed to say relatively little, have rather bland office decor, and even not take public political stands (Greenson 1967). Furthermore, this nongratifying attitude of the therapist, by subtly depriving the patient, was thought to increase the transference. Finally, the blankness of the therapist was supposed to aid in the patient's understanding of the transference, once the therapist pointed it out.

Currently many therapists feel that the transference will develop strongly regardless of the therapist's activity level. Furthermore, transference has come increasingly to be regarded as a creation of both patient and therapist. The artificiality of a bland and silent therapist is counterproductive.

Transference is also used loosely to describe the entire relationship between therapist and patient. For example, a supervisor might ask a therapist what is happening in the transference with the patient, meaning all aspects of the therapeutic relationship as well as the patient's distortions of the therapist.

Transference is an extremely complex and profound concept. Different understandings of transference make up some of the major differences between various schools of psychotherapy. We will discuss dealing with the transference more in Chapter 11.

The complex intertwining of transference with other aspects of human experience can be illustrated in the following situation. First, a man with an ambivalent relationship to his mother chooses a wife somewhat like his mother. Second, he then perceives her to have some traits similar to his mother in areas where she does not (transference). Third, he acts in such a way (unconsciously) as to induce her to act toward him in ways like his mother did (role induction, Sandler 1976). With his therapist, this man may repeat the second and third patterns, which, it is hoped, can be understood in the work.

COUNTERTRANSFERENCE

The term *countertransference* is generally used in two different ways. In the *narrow* usage, it means the therapist's transference to the patient. Used in this sense, countertransference means the therapist's distortion of the patient, based on coloration from the therapist's own past. Thus, a therapist might have trouble empathizing with a controlling but depressed female patient, who unconsciously reminds him of his mother. He might be unmoved by the patient's suffering, he might be overly afraid of her hostility, he might be too confronting or not confronting enough. The therapist may be unaware of these reactions within himself.

Countertransference used in its *broad* sense refers to all the feelings of the therapist toward the patient, conscious and unconscious. This usage is particularly prevalent in British journals and in other journals published outside of the United States. Recently, however, this broader use is gaining ever wider acceptance.

Countertransference in its broad sense thus applies to therapists' feelings of affection, disappointment, idealization, anger, love, disgust, and so on toward their patients, and also includes all the fantasies a therapist might have about his patients. The therapeutic use of countertransference will be discussed in Chapter 11.

DEFENSE MECHANISMS

This term refers to a long list of processes within the mind. Generally, *defense* refers to a person's attempt to avoid anxiety. (*Anxiety* can be defined as a kind of psychological fear, often accompanied by physical manifestations, such as sweating and an increased heart rate.) Sometimes other painful emotions, such as guilt, sadness, or shame, are also the objects of defenses.

Examples of defense mechanisms are *repression*, *displacement*, *reaction formation*, *projection*, *isolation of affect*, *undoing*, and *rationalization*, as well as many others (Anna Freud 1936). The use of these mechanisms, which occurs to some extent in all human beings, entails some disturbance of a person's sense of reality. These specific mechanisms are defined in all textbooks of psychopathology and abnormal psychology. The important thing at this point is understanding that the defenses are against painful inner states, primarily anxiety.

RESISTANCE

Technically, *resistance* refers to the action of forces within a person that oppose the work of therapy, that oppose change. Resistance can take the form of a patient not wanting to talk about sensitive subjects, not remembering any dreams, forgetting to come to a therapy session, or even quitting therapy.

This term is widely misunderstood. All too often therapists either blame the patient for having resistances, or feel that the patient should not have them. *Resistances represent a patient's attempts to protect himself or herself.* Just as defenses are necessary to the personality in daily life, so resistances are necessary in therapy. There is always a part of each patient that wants to work with the therapist and to change. And there is always another part of each patient that is afraid of change, does not want to change, and will work against the therapist. At different times one or another of these parts will be weaker or stronger.

In fact, there is no therapy without resistance. To some degree, it is present in every therapy hour, from the first to the last. Working with resistance is a major part of psychotherapeutic work. It is the therapist's job to understand the motivation for the resistance. Why is the patient avoiding a sensitive subject? What are his or her fears? Why does it seem like a good idea not to talk about it?

Resistances are often unconscious. A patient may forget a therapy hour because of something painful that surfaced in the previous hour, or because the therapist said something hurtful, or because the therapist is going on vacation. Even if the patient does not agree that forgetting the hour was purposeful, dealing with the painful events of a previous hour, or with the therapist's impending vacation, will help the therapy progress and may prevent future "no shows."

Conscious or unconscious, resistances must be dealt with sooner or later. A well-known teacher of psychotherapy was famous for repeatedly entreating his students, "Process the resistance! Process the resistance!"

Because of the tendency of therapists to blame patients for having resistances, it is sometimes argued that the term should be dropped. However, a therapist who understands the concept will be able to deal with so-called negative attitudes of patients.

P: I think that therapy is a crock.

T: Yes, I do too sometimes. Perhaps you are scared that our working together might turn out to be a crock.

It is fairly common for adolescents not to want to come to therapy.

P (16 years old): I don't need to be here, and I'm not going to talk to you.

T: Well, I certainly can't force you to talk. On the other hand your parents are paying me so I'm here. I'm interested in why they sent you if you don't need to come.

P: My grades have gone down and they think I'm depressed.

The adolescent in the above example loosened up fairly quickly. However, if an adolescent shows up for his or her session, the therapist can infer that there is some wish for help and change. As long as any patient appears for his or her hour, it is naive for the therapist to conclude with finality, "The patient just doesn't want to work." As a sort of worst-case scenario, it is possible that a patient could have as his or her primary agenda to remain unchanged and to discredit the therapist. However, that could be discovered only after considerable work, and even then the patient would have other contradictory motives within.

The notion that a conscious wish for therapy is not always required for therapeutic change to occur (for example, with adolescents) has some interesting implications. Since therapy consists of an interaction between two people that is helpful to one of them, therapeutic processes or events could occur between two people regardless of the patient's desire for treatment. It might not even matter who is defined as the patient, or whether or not the relationship is defined as therapy. A noted psychologist (Kaiser 1962) wrote a play, "Emergency," about a paranoid psychiatrist who refused to seek therapeutic help. His wife hired another psychiatrist to treat her husband by going to him as a patient! In his role as a patient, the second psychiatrist was able to create interactions helpful to the sick psychiatrist!

In summary, resistance needs to be understood by the therapist like anything else of significance that occurs in the therapy.

INTERPRETATION

Interpretation occupies a central place in insight psycho-therapy. Succinctly, the aim of interpretation is to *make the unconscious conscious*. This includes unconscious feelings, fantasies, memories, and behavior patterns.

The therapist helped the timid assistant plant manager to become aware of the (previously unconscious) intensity of his anger at his boss. Later, the therapist helped the manager understand his feelings toward his father, and his general mode of passivity in relation to authority.

Through her therapy, the woman who had married three alcoholic husbands gradually became aware of the connection between her feelings toward her father and her choice of men. Later, she became aware of her deeply ambivalent feelings toward both of her parents. Finally, she was able to change her pattern of self-defeating behavior in relationships so that she could get more of what she wanted and needed from a relationship with a man.

The changes in these patients occurred gradually, through a series of interpretations made by their therapists. Sometimes the therapist pointed out a feeling that seemed to be hidden within the patient, such as sadness or anger. Sometimes the therapist speculated that the patient might have a specific unconscious wish or fantasy, such as a wish to attack someone. At other times the therapist stated that there seemed to be a recurring pattern in the patient's behavior. All of these interventions represent different forms of interpretation.

Greenson (1967) divides the process of interpretation into four stages. These are (1) confrontation, (2) clarification, (3) interpretation, and (4) working through. Frequently one or more of these stages are combined.

An example of *confrontation* is the therapist pointing out to a patient an aspect of behavior that he was unaware of— for instance, the timid plant manager's extreme subservience to his boss. (In this case, the patient was already partly aware of this pattern.)

Clarification entails a discussion of the details, including how much and how often the patient behaved in this way.

The therapist then *interprets* the strength of the patient's anger toward his boss and his father. Further interpretations are directed toward his fear of his aggression toward these figures, his long-suppressed longing for his father's love, as well as other feelings and fantasies toward authority figures.

The process of *working through* consists of the patient's reaction to the therapist's comments, and the patient's use of these insights in making constructive life changes. Working through entails the integration of insight into the patient's life. Greenson considers this fourth stage of interpretation, working through, to require the longest period of time.

We will discuss more about interpretation in Chapter 11.

PSYCHIC STRUCTURE

The use of this term is sometimes confusing. Essentially it means aspects of the mind and its functioning that do not change, or change only very slowly, over time. Thus the terms *ego* or the *unconscious*, when they are referred to as structures of the mind, mean functions or places in the mind that are stable over time.

There is another meaning, however, familiar to all experienced therapists. This is the sense in which the psychic structure of the patient's mind is like a parking structure, made of cement—hard, rigid, and immovable. Thus it requires a great deal of effort from both patient and therapist to change it. Understanding this folk wisdom may help a therapist not to become discouraged when progress seems slow.

The above use of the word *structure* is not to be confused with the *structural theory* of Freud, in which the functions of the mind are divided into the id, ego, and superego. In Freudian psychology the structural theory superseded the earlier model of the mind called the *topographic theory*, which divided the mind into the conscious, preconscious, and unconscious.

CHAPTER 8

A Comparison of Friendship, Supportive Psychotherapy, and Insight Psychotherapy

- Goals
- Therapist rewards
- Transference
- Self-revelation by the therapist
- Use of suggestion
- Direction/focus
- Time limitation
- Nature of frame

This book is primarily about *insight psychotherapy* (which, as mentioned previously, is roughly synonymous with psychoanalytically oriented psychotherapy, long-term psychotherapy, depth psychotherapy, and psychodynamic psychotherapy). This type of treatment is suitable for most neurotic patients and many borderline and narcissistic patients (including those with so-called personality disorders). It is generally not suitable for psychotics, true sociopaths, some adolescents, in situations where there is an extreme crisis, or where there are limited treatment resources (such as in a clinic that severely restricts the number of sessions).

To aid in understanding the nature of insight therapy, it is useful to compare it with supportive psychotherapy and friendship in a number of different aspects.

Supportive psychotherapy is generally used for more disturbed patients such as schizophrenics or severe borderlines, especially those with "complicating factors such as inadequate education, unstable financial support systems, substance abuse, or severe eating disorders" (Rockland 1989, p. 5). It is also useful for some adolescents, as well as for other patients who for one reason or anther are not suited for insight therapy.

Supportive psychotherapy techniques blend into those used for crisis intervention—for example, focusing on only one problem at a time or on areas related to a current crisis. Its goals are also similar to those used in crisis counseling— coping with immediate crises and problems, restoring a previous level of functioning, and preventing deterioration.

In supportive psychotherapy the therapist does not make interpretations of the patient's unconscious. Instead the therapist attempts (1) to support and strengthen the patient's existing strengths and coping skills, (2) to help the patient deal concretely with reality issues, and (3) to enhance the patient's self-esteem through the relationship with the therapist. By being more "real" the therapist hopes to discourage the formation of transference, and provide a human relationship and example for the patient. There are many similarities between supportive psychotherapy and what is sometimes called relationship therapy.

Friendship has significant contrasting elements when compared with both insight and supportive psychotherapy.

Table 8–1 summarizes the comparison of friendship, supportive psychotherapy, and insight psychotherapy in eight different categories.

GOALS

The goals of friendship include companionship, the sharing of both happiness and sorrow, mutual support, loyalty, and

Table 8–1
A Comparison of Friendship, Supportive Psychotherapy, and
Insight Psychotherapy

	Friendship	*Supportive Therapy*	*Insight Therapy*
Goals	Variable	Immediate functioning	Awareness/growth
Therapist rewards	Variable	Pride/money	Pride/money
Transference	Silent	Discouraged	Encouraged and interpreted
Self-revelation by the therapist	Frequent	Flexible	Minimal
Use of suggestion	Frequent	Flexible	Minimal
Direction/focus	Unlimited	Focused	Open-ended
Time limitation	Unlimited	Limited or unlimited	Related to process
Nature of frame	Loose	Somewhat flexible	Minimally flexible

advice. Other goals may include hero worship, a "mutual admiration society," or sexual union.

Often the goals of friendship are unspoken or even unconscious. The relationship between friends may be approximately equal or decidedly one-sided. Nevertheless, there is always something in it for each party. This is put starkly by Friedman (1988) who wrote, "Two people alone with nothing to do will exploit each other." Due to the complexity of human beings and the myriad forms of relationships, the goals of friendship are extremely variable.

The goals of supportive psychotherapy, as described above, generally focus on dealing with immediate reality.

The goals of insight psychotherapy are sometimes described as structural change, meaning lasting changes in the personality. However, these goals also can be stated succinctly as awareness and growth. *Awareness* relates to insight into oneself and the accurate assessment of external reality. *Growth* occurs as a result of the use of insight and the relationship with the therapist.

THERAPIST REWARDS

The legitimate rewards for the psychotherapist are more or less limited to two. The first is a complex mixture of joy in the growth of the patient, pleasure in being a part of that growth, and satisfaction in the exercise of a fine craft. A pleasurable aspect of this craft is enjoying the unique stimulation it provides. I have chosen the word *pride*, as in pride in one's work, to sum up this complex experience.

The second reward for therapists is money. Doing therapy is hard work. The therapist's unflagging concentration on understanding the patient throughout each session is both demanding and unique. Therapists need to be paid and to learn to accept their fees without guilt.

Over the years, I have occasionally heard the opinion expressed that a patient needs to pay for therapy in order for it to be effective. Not only has this been contrary to my observations and experience, but it is theoretically naive. If a patient's not having to pay for therapy becomes a resistance (for example, in the case of a welfare patient on Medicaid), then that needs to be dealt with in the therapy.

> T: You were telling me that neither the kids in public schools nor their teachers try very hard. You are frequently late for our sessions. Are you having some feelings about our therapy because it's free?
>
> P: Well . . .
>
> T: Maybe you feel you get what you pay for?
>
> P: Maybe that's true.
>
> T: Perhaps you don't feel you deserve to benefit from our work. You have told me you felt worthless and defeated.
>
> P: Yes. I still feel that way. Sometimes, everything seems so hard.
>
> T: I'd like to hear more about that.

In all worthwhile lines of work there can be found practitioners who work only for the pleasure of it—for example, volunteer policemen, teachers, seamstresses, lawyers, and gardeners, to name only a few. Therapists (and supervisors) who volunteer their time are no exception.

Understanding the legitimate rewards for the therapist is important because there are so many opportunities for the intrusion of other gratifications into the therapy situation. For example, if a therapist has a need for his patients to like or admire him, he will influence his patients to do that. To begin with, most patients want to please their therapists, whom they see as powerful authority figures. Next, the therapist will selectively reinforce the patient's adulatory behavior. As a result, patients may not feel free to express disappointment or frustration with the therapy, nor to voice their reactions to the therapist's shortcomings and errors.

Consciously or unconsciously, a therapist may wish to be liked, admired, entertained, stimulated, titillated, involved in dramatic situations, or even attacked by the patient. The therapist may also need for the patient *not* to express angry, homosexual, or suicidal feelings. In each of these cases the therapist will subtly coerce the patient into fulfilling the therapist's agenda, rather than the patient's own path toward growth.

Between friends, praise, gifts, sex, and love can be given freely and accepted at face value. It is only in the unique situation of psychotherapy that these interactions necessarily come under scrutiny. However, only by constant attention can therapists prevent their desires from subverting their daily work.

These limitations on rewards apply both to supportive and insight psychotherapists. However, in supportive therapy it is sometimes useful for the patient to do things for the therapist, for example, bringing food for the therapist or sharing music tapes. In these situations the therapist must be genuinely pleased, but not too attached to the gifts or services.

Deep motivations (with consequent rewards) are undoubtedly satisfied by being a therapist. An expanded discussion of the rewards offered by the career of psychotherapy is presented in Chapter 17.

TRANSFERENCE

In friendship, transference occurs regularly, but is usually unrecognized—most people believe they perceive others accurately.

In supportive psychotherapy, the therapist attempts to minimize the development of transference by endeavoring for the patient to see him or her as a real person. This is because many patients for whom supportive psychotherapy is suitable tend to form transferences that are too intense to be worked with. Furthermore, the transferences of severe borderline or schizophrenic patients are often accompanied by regression and a worsening of symptoms. In some cases, however, already regressed psychotic patients are helped by a stable relationship with their benign, loving, idealized "doctor." Instead of interpreting transference, the supportive psychotherapist attempts to exploit the positive transference, while offering a committed, human relationship.

The therapeutic use of transference—its formation and interpretation—is a central feature of insight psychotherapy. By an empathic yet nonintrusive stance the insight therapist encourages the development of transference. It is then interpreted to help the patient understand how he creates the interpersonal world that he experiences as objective, given reality. This important subject is dealt with in more detail in Chapter 11.

SELF-REVELATION BY THE THERAPIST

Friends usually reveal many of their experiences and feelings to each other.

Supportive psychotherapists vary in how much they share their own experiences and feelings with patients. With some patients, the therapist's revealing herself can promote trust, intimacy, the accurate appraisal of reality, and enhance the patient's self-esteem. The more the therapist feels that an honest, human relationship will benefit the patient, the more she will self-disclose, as she would with a friend. However, the disadvantages of self-revelation for insight therapy can also occur in supportive psychotherapy.

In insight therapy self-revelation by the therapist is fraught with difficulties, but it is often attempted for therapeutic reasons. For example, the therapist may wish to lessen the patient's self-criticism and low self-esteem by offering examples of her own fallibility.

> T: Don't feel so bad about being fired. It happened to me once.

Or the therapist may wish to encourage the patient.

> T: Yes, divorces are horribly difficult. It took me years to recover from mine.

The therapist may feel that answering a patient's question directly is both innocuous and will promote the relationship.

> P: Do you have children?
> T: Yes, I have three sons.

Other reasons that therapists self-disclose are attempts to reassure the patient.

> T: Yes, I do care about you.
> Or a therapist may feel that she should tell the patient if she feels angry at him, in order to be "real" or authentic, to validate his suspicions, or to let him know that his behavior is provocative.

T: I felt angry at you for canceling your appointment at the last minute.

The problem with these interventions is that it is impossible to be sure that the intended beneficial effects will occur. For example, the therapist's revealing that she was fired once, supposedly just like the patient, may be experienced by the patient as a mocking attack. The patient may feel, "Yes, you got fired once, and look at you now. You've got it together while I'm a blubbering mess. I'm sure you didn't fall apart like I'm doing." Even if the therapist insists that she was devastated the patient may not believe her. Or the patient may feel a need to comfort the therapist:

P: What happened? It must have been a really difficult time for you.

The patient may have a similar response to hearing about the therapist's divorce, thinking, "Yes, yours was probably mutually agreed on, and there weren't any money problems." Or the patient may feel, "Maybe you don't know how to make a relationship work either. How can you help me, then?"

By directly answering a patient's question about how many children she has, the therapist may fail to understand the deeper meaning of the patient's question. For example, the patient may want to know if the therapist can understand the difficulties he is having with his teenage daughter. In this case, the therapist might accomplish more by an inquiring attitude.

P: Do you have children?

T: Perhaps you're wondering if I can understand what it's like to have children?

P: Yes, my 13-year-old daughter may be pregnant.

A therapist who tells her patient she cares for him might be setting up a recurrent need for reassurance: "Now that I've told you something worse about me," the patient might ask, "do you still care about me?" Furthermore, patients sometimes misinterpret direct expressions of emotion by the therapist. "I care about you," might be heard as, "I love you."

A therapist who tells her patient that she is angry at him for canceling a session runs the risk of scaring him. He might respond with brittle compliance, but then feel less free to express himself. He might abruptly quit therapy.

Self-disclosure by the therapist might have its intended effect or it might miscarry in unpredictable ways. Moreover, the therapist might not sense and the patient might not tell the therapist of its negative effects.

If the therapist understands what she is trying to accomplish by self-disclosure, she might be able to find other ways to accomplish it. For example, regarding the patient's harsh self-criticism connected with being fired, the therapist could point out the patient's extremely harsh attitude toward himself, and his expectation that the therapist will feel contemptuous.

Regarding a divorced patient who is discouraged, the therapist could point out that it generally takes people a long time to recover from a divorce, but that most people do make new relationships eventually. The therapist could then ask the patient to list his strengths. (Of course, the therapist's *being with* the patient in his grief over his divorce is also crucial. This topic is explored further in Chapters 13 and 14.)

When a patient asks the therapist if she likes him or cares about him, or accuses her of not caring, the therapist could inquire about why the patient is asking this now. What makes the patient feel that the therapist does not care? Does the patient feel that he is likable or worth caring about? Sometimes it is useful for the therapist to say,

T: One of the reasons you came into therapy was because you felt insecure. Maybe it's important for you to learn to know for yourself if you are worthwhile rather than have me tell you.

A therapist who thinks of telling the patient that she is angry at him for canceling his appointment might be better off inquiring into the multiple reasons why he canceled.

T: What led to your canceling the appointment?

P: I had to study for a final exam.

T: What else?

P: Well, I'm not sure it's helping me very much to come here.

T: Tell me more about that.

Finally, in contrast with other techniques, self-disclosure by the therapist is particularly likely to contain hidden agendas of the therapist. For example, the therapist may have an unrecognized inner need to ask the patient to help her!

THE USE OF SUGGESTION

Friends often give each other advice. In psychotherapy the use of advice or suggestion is a complex matter, as described above.

Supportive psychotherapists often give advice to their patients. Examples include:

Take your medications.

Go to AA (Alcoholics Anonymous).

Contact the State Department of Vocational Rehabilitation.

Take one class in school.

Maybe you'll sleep better if you don't worry about that problem.

Chances are, everything will settle down and you'll be fine.

Even though giving advice is relatively common in supportive psychotherapy, the maxim from crisis intervention applies: "Don't do anything for the patient that the patient can do for himself."

In insight psychotherapy, the therapist tries to avoid the use of suggestion as much as possible.

DIRECTION AND FOCUS

Friends discuss whatever subjects they wish.

In supportive psychotherapy, the therapist helps the patient focus on a limited number of specific problems or issues. In this sense the therapist directs the patient, keeping him on track. The therapist also may direct the patient away from difficult, unconscious material, for example, the meaning of some dreams. The supportive psychotherapist keeps this focus in mind, even though she may listen attentively to anything the patient wishes to tell her.

In contrast, insight therapy is open ended. The therapist will listen and then attempt to deal with whatever the patient brings to the hour. In her choice of what to comment upon, the therapist tries not to limit the patient's freedom to explore all aspects of himself.

TIME LIMITATION

Friendship has no time limitations.

Supportive psychotherapy may have external time limitations. For example, clinic rules may limit the number of sessions, or a therapist may only be assigned to a clinic for a specific time period. Some therapists will limit the time of therapy for theoretical reasons (for example, various forms of brief or short-term psychotherapy). In other situations, the therapist may need to see the patient for life, for example, to provide an ongoing, stable contact for an extremely isolated person, or to prevent a seriously disturbed person from deteriorating.

In insight work, the length of the therapy is related to the process itself. Ordinarily the therapy ends when the goals of the patient have been reached, or when the patient and therapist agree that they have reached a good stopping point. A course of insight therapy can be as short as a few months or as long as many years. However, it is important that there be a planned ending. Significant developments usually occur during the ending phase. It is also important for the patient to have time afterward without therapy to integrate the experience.

NATURE OF THE FRAME

The *frame* in psychotherapy refers to the relatively fixed arrangements of the therapy situation and the attitudes of the therapist. It is somewhat like a picture frame, which contains and surrounds the canvas on which *anything*—beautiful or ugly, organized or chaotic—may be painted. The frame includes physical arrangements, such as the configuration of the therapist's office, the set fee, hours, and length of sessions, and the exclusive one-to-one relationship, with total confidentiality. It also includes the role of the therapist, who does not cross certain boundaries, even if invited, and who steadily honors her commitment to help the patient by means of understanding and the communication of that understanding (interpretation) (Langs 1977).

Friendships may have a frame, such as the prohibition of

theft or adultery, but ordinarily the frame for friendships is rather flexible and certainly may change over time.

In supportive psychotherapy the frame is less flexible. The therapist may relax some boundaries, and do many things other than communicate understanding, but the commitment to helping the patient as the raison d'être for the entire relationship (which is a significant part of the frame) is unwavering.

In insight psychotherapy the frame should be minimally flexible. Even when it is aggressively challenged by the patient, the therapist's constancy may be unconsciously reassuring.

> A patient asked his therapist to accept stock in his start-up company as payment in lieu of cash. (If the therapist had accepted, she might have subtly encouraged the patient to work harder!)

> A female patient declared her love for her male therapist and suggested they have sex during the therapy hours.

> A patient demanded that the therapist be available for telephone sessions at any time, day or night.

In each of these situations the therapist did not act as the patient urged, but was able to work with the patient in a way that ultimately proved to be helpful. The therapist always needs to evaluate each situation carefully, and to explore the meanings of the patient's experience. These situations are among the most difficult problems in psychotherapy, and specific examples will be discussed in Chapters 10 and 11.

MORE ON THE GOALS OF INSIGHT PSYCHOTHERAPY

Insight therapy addresses itself to the goals of the patient. Directly or indirectly, the therapist asks the patient, "What do you want?'' Responses may include success at work, a romantic relationship, to feel less depressed, or something as vague as "to be happy." As emphasized throughout this book, the therapist will then attempt to understand the patient, his goals, and the difficulties he has achieving them. What does it mean for the patient to be "happy"? What has happened so far in the patient's attempts to achieve this? And so forth.

What the patient wants needs to remain continually in the therapist's focus. However, the patient's conscious goals can (and often do) change during the course of the work. A patient may start off by wanting to feel less depressed, then progress to issues involving both work and relationships.

It has been said that all any therapist can do, in even the most complex and lengthy therapy, is to help the patient to have more choices. In insight therapy this is accomplished by helping the patient to be more aware of both internal and external reality. It is for this reason that a central goal of insight therapy is *awareness*.

CHAPTER 9

The Opening Phase of Psychotherapy

- Two goals of the opening phase
- What to do first
- The fear of regression

The first goal of the opening phase is building a relationship with the patient. This process depends on the therapist's emotional contact with the patient. For most people, going to a therapist is a scary experience. Probably everyone feels uneasy talking about their inner feelings, especially to a stranger. Additionally, each new patient has his own particular issues—feeling ashamed of something, guilty and afraid of being judged, and so on. The therapist needs to monitor the patient's experience as sensitively as possible.

If the therapist is able to set the patient at ease, the early work may progress smoothly as the patient unburdens himself. Or the patient may develop uncomfortable feelings or suspicions. Particular attention should be paid to the patient's fears and resistances. Responding to these will foster the relationship. For example:

> P: I've felt like I was on my own ever since I can remember, and it's true, no matter what anybody says, you have to do things on your own.

T: Maybe you wonder if this therapy can help you. Maybe you wonder if anyone can help you. It doesn't sound like you've had the experience of another person being with you emotionally.

Or,

P: (At the end of a session) You haven't given me any feedback today.

T: It's true that I haven't said much today. At the beginning of our work I may not have much to say, because I'm still getting to know you. I think what you've told me about yourself today is very important.

If there was still some time left in the session for the patient to respond, the therapist might add:

T: Maybe you wonder if I'll ever have any helpful comments.

● The issue of trust frequently arises in the early hours.

P: I know I need to trust you as my therapist.

T: Hopefully that will develop as we go along. But I'm sure you know that not all professionals are trustworthy. You'll have to use your own judgment to discover for yourself whether or not I'm trustworthy.

● The second goal of the opening phase is arousing the patient's curiosity about himself or herself—initiating a process of self-observation, along with a sense of collaboration with the therapist. One example was described to me by a colleague. Her patient, an abrasive entrepreneur, had complained that his co-workers called him obnoxious.

> T: I know you think that talking to a therapist is a lot of bull, but aren't you even the least, tiny bit curious about what makes people think that about you?
>
> P: (After a pause) I would like to come back next week.

Just as the therapist observes the patient and points out patterns or makes interpretations, the patient is invited to observe himself or herself. In a sense the therapist is always working to develop this capacity in the patient, but it is especially important in the early phases.

> T: From what you tell me, you seem to become infatuated on every first date.
>
> P: Yes. I was thinking that that happened again last weekend.
>
> T: I'm glad you can make that kind of observation for yourself.

Another example:

> T: What do you make of your getting anxiety attacks at work?
>
> P: I don't know.
>
> T: Well, there must be something significant bothering you. At this point we're both mystified.

If these twin goals, (1) building a relationship and (2) initiating a process of self-observation, are achieved, the process of the patient and therapist working together will have achieved a good start.

Informally, some therapists think of "hooking the patient" as a goal of the opening phase. By this they mean involving the patient in the treatment process enough so that he will continue to come. In this regard, therapists find themselves pulled two ways. On the one hand, the therapist would like to emphasize the benefits of treatment. On the other, it is important for the therapist not to be a salesman. The therapist needs to support the patient's freedom of choice and his ability to sense what is best for him. The best way to show a hesitant patient the benefits of treatment is to begin working to understand him, for example by identifying his fears and the pros and cons of treatment in his own mind.

WHAT TO DO FIRST

Some therapists like to explain free association to the patient—as his or her role—in the first few meetings.

> T: I would like for you to tell me whatever occurs to you. In ordinary social conversations, people censor what they say. I'd like for you to try not to do that here. Feel free to tell me anything—a thought, a feeling, a memory, a bodily sensation, or a dream. Here are some of the reasons people often censor: One, I think it's trivial. Two, I've said it before. Three, what will he think of me if I say *that*?

Of course, a therapist could say only part of the above, such as:

> T: Just talk about whatever comes to mind.

In psychoanalysis, free association is called the *basic rule*, which the patient is urged to follow. However, it is also said that when a patient can truly free associate, his analysis is completed. True free association is probably impossible for a variety of reasons, including the fact that people can think faster than they can talk.

It is striking that therapy is the only place in the world where a person can say anything he wants. Commenting on this fascinating observation, Ekstein (1983) added, "No society in history has ever allowed that."

Many therapists never tell their patients to free associate, but simply try to deal with whatever the patient brings up. If the patient asks what he should talk about, the therapist might reply,

> T: Talk about what bothers you.

The problem with this response is that it implies that the patient should not tell the therapist about a wonderful success he has just had. Other therapists say,

> T: Whatever your mind wants to bring up will be a fine place to start.

or,

> T: Let's both trust that your mind will bring up things for us to talk about.

Or a therapist could approach the patient's question about what to discuss as a resistance:

> T: Maybe your concern about what to talk about is part of the fear that you can't do this, and that I can't help you.

Silence can occur in any phase of therapy, but perhaps it is most difficult in the opening phase. Inexperienced therapists are often uncomfortable with silence, and hesitate to let it go on for more than a few seconds.

There are many ways to deal with silence. A venerable therapist was once asked how she dealt with silence. She replied, "I listen to the silence." Silence is often useful in therapy. A patient can mull over a new insight, collect himself after a catharsis, or gather up his courage, secure in the knowledge of his therapist's calm attentiveness.

If the therapist wishes to interrupt a silence, some of the following may prove useful:

○ T: What are you experiencing?

This is less restrictive than

T: What are you thinking?

or

T: What are you feeling?

although at specific times, it may be better to ask one of these latter questions.

Other options for the therapist include:

T: I notice that you're silent. Where did you go?

T: You look depressed [or bored or sad or angry].

T: Is there something you are avoiding?

T: I'm here. Whenever you're able [or willing] to tell me something . . .

○ If a long silence has occurred, what the patient says spontaneously at the end of it may be especially important.

○ There are two basic areas that a therapist can focus on, whenever he or she does not know what to do. The first of these is *affect* (feelings). In fact, it is almost a maxim: *When in doubt, go for affect.* One way to do this might be to describe the patient's strongest affect in the session so far:

> T: You showed considerable anger a few minutes ago.

or,

> T: I sensed some sadness when you were discussing . . .

An exception to this would be when working with a patient who is overwhelmed by too much feeling. This type of patient needs to be helped to think and reflect.

Affect is important because we "live" in our feelings. This is reflected not only in the ubiquitous, social, "How do you feel today?" but by the nature of the word *feelings* itself. To a significant degree, we are what we feel. Happiness, sadness, worry, anger, disappointment, shame, joy, puzzlement, all reflect states that are of immediate importance to individuals.

A person is less likely to fool himself with feelings than with thoughts. As Semrad (Rako and Mazer 1980) put it,

> If you feel like crying, you cry. You see, there's one thing you can depend on, and that's the autonomic nervous system. It never lies. It's so far from the head it doesn't even know there is a head. [p. 27]

More succinctly, Semrad added, "Tears never lie in a male" (p. 163). Even if there is supposedly no reason for a feeling, it is nevertheless important and meaningful.

Here is a commonplace example of feelings being wiser than thoughts:

> P: I feel down today, but I don't know why. I don't think I should be feeling this way, because everything is going very well.

T: Feelings always have meaning. (Pause) I believe you told me that something happened on today's date.

P: I'd forgotten. My mother died five years ago today!

Another example:

P: I didn't want to come to see you today, but I don't know why. I usually look forward to coming.

T: Perhaps you felt cut off at the end of our last session. You were in the midst of telling me something very important.

P: Now that you bring it up, I did feel you ended the session abruptly.

How do you feel about that? is one of the questions therapists ask most frequently. Feelings can be explored in relation to nearly everything a patient brings up—the present, the past, and the relationship with the therapist (the transference).

When a feeling is identified and experienced vividly by the patient, the therapist may wonder what to do next. Often the best thing to do is to wait, especially if the therapist feels "in sync" with the patient. Other tacks for the therapist include:

T: Perhaps it's scary to feel so strongly.

T: What does this feeling remind you of?

T: When have you experienced this feeling before?

A different issue arises if a patient does not experience a feeling vividly. Then the therapist might comment:

T: You say you feel angry, but you don't look very upset.

or,

> T: You're describing a sad situation, but you seem to be smiling. (Not: Why are you smiling?)

Alternatively, the therapist might ask a patient to describe his feeling more completely.

> P: It really made me mad when he did that.
> T: What's that feeling like?

It is also useful to ask a patient where in his body he experiences a feeling, as a way of helping him become more in touch with himself. Another way of approaching feelings is by asking the patient to describe his angry or shameful or lustful fantasies (assuming the feeling has already been mentioned).

As with any other rules for doing therapy, there are exceptions. Some affects or fantasies are too painful, frightening, or full of shame for a patient to deal with at the beginning of therapy. There is no substitute for sensitivity in the therapist.

Semrad (Rako and Mazer 1980) commented on the importance of dealing with feelings in therapy:

> Go after what the patient feels and cannot do himself. Help him to acknowledge what he cannot bear himself, and stay with him until he can stand it. [p. 105]

The second basic area for a therapist to focus on is exploration. Semrad (Rako and Mazer 1980) advised, "Whenever you don't know what to do: investigate" (p. 110). Furthermore, he emphasized his point: "Investigate, investigate, investigate" (p. 110).

This need for a therapist to investigate further is obvious when a patient volunteers no more than his sex life is "fine."

However, it is equally necessary in less obvious situations. For example, a patient might say that he is a nuclear physicist. If more about his job were not forthcoming from the patient, the therapist might ask the patient what he actually does during the day, whom he works with and for, what are the rewards and drawbacks of his career, how much does he make, and so on. In these details reside the real experience of the patient's life that the therapist needs to understand. Another approach might be:

T: Help me understand what your workday is like.

Supervisors often need to prompt beginning therapists to investigate more deeply, as in these examples:

Supervisor to therapist: What does the patient mean when she says her mother was overprotective? Try to get her to give you examples.

Supervisor: How did the patient know her father was an alcoholic? Was he an angry drunk or did he withdraw?

Supervisor: When your patient says he thought about you between sessions, what did he think? What are his fantasies?

TWO RELIABLE INDICATORS
OF THERAPEUTIC PROGRESS

Affect and exploration are useful, not only as avenues for the therapist to pursue, but also as reliable indicators of therapeutic progress.

If a patient is experiencing feelings in the presence of the therapist, it is generally a sign that the therapy is moving forward. One reason to call this progress is that most patients did not have their feelings validated or even recognized during their formative years. Thus they became alienated from themselves. The experiencing of feelings in the presence of an empathic therapist is healing. It gives the patient back himself. (Exceptions to this are patients who experience too much feeling without the capacity to think or reflect. In these patients progress can be measured by increases in reality testing and self-observation.)

Hearing new material is another reliable sign of progress. This new material may be about the present or the past, and in many cases may include dreams (see Chapter 12). Not only is the therapist learning more about the patient and his world, but when a patient tells something new to the therapist, he is also telling himself in some way. This sign is even more encouraging if the new information has significant emotional content.

THINKING VERSUS FEELING VERSUS ACTION

Early in therapy many patients are unable to distinguish *thoughts* from *feelings*.

T: How do you feel about your wife leaving you?

P: I feel she shouldn't have left.

T: It seems hard for you to express your feelings directly. I guess they're pretty painful.

At this juncture, the patient might start to cry, or he might simply repeat his statement that she shouldn't have left, it was her duty to stay, they were married in the church, and so on. In extreme cases, a person is unable to recognize feelings at all, a condition called *alexithymia*. Such patients are sometimes more suited to supportive therapy rather than insight therapy.

Sometimes a direct confrontation by the therapist is helpful.

> T: I ask you what you feel, and you tell me what you think. How do you *feel* about her leaving?

The difference between *feelings* and *actions* is even more important, and recognizing this difference represents an important therapeutic gain for some patients.

> P: I'm afraid I'm going to get angry with my parents.
>
> T: Do you mean that you will *feel* angry with them or *act* angry?
>
> P: What's the difference?
>
> T: There is an important difference between feelings and actions. You might feel angry, but decide not to say anything, not to act on it. Or you might decide to tell them off. That would certainly be an action. It's possible to feel strong feelings without having to act on them.

The following situation occurred in the therapy of a 14-year-old girl:

> P: When I feel sexy with a boy, we do something about it.
>
> T: What do you think would happen if you allowed yourself just to feel those feelings, without acting on them?

Many patients do not recognize the feeling of anxiety.

A man who claimed he was "oversexed" did not recognize his intense anxiety about emotional closeness with a woman. He covered over his fears with compulsive sexual activity. Only after several discussions with his therapist was he able to admit to feeling anxious just being with and talking to a woman.

Addictive behaviors frequently mask anxiety.

> T: What do you feel, just before you take that first drink that leads to a bender?
> P: I think I'll just have a drink to relax.
> T: Do you recognize that you are tense at that time?
> P: No. Well, maybe a little.
> T: I think you are very anxious in social situations, but that you don't recognize the feeling of anxiety. If you learned to recognize it, maybe we could work together on other ways of coping with it besides drinking.

Patients benefit by learning to describe their feelings in words. In turn, they can learn to tolerate these feelings without having to act, and therefore can make better choices.

SOME TIME-HONORED RULES

There are a few time-honored technical rules for insight psychotherapy. These apply to all phases, but may be especially useful in the opening phase. First, deal with *resistance before content*. An example might involve a patient with a painful memory about something he feels shameful about. The content is the memory. The resistance is the reluctance the patient feels about revealing feelings of pain and shame.

Following the above recommendation, the therapist might ask the patient what his shame is about. Does he feel the therapist would judge him if he revealed himself? Would the patient feel critical if a friend told him of a similar experience? Does the patient feel that whatever led him to that experience was *understandable*?

Above all, the therapist should be respectful of the patient's struggle. It may be useful to ask,

> T: Do you feel it's okay if you *don't* tell me right now?

Sometimes a patient guards a "secret." The therapist needs to approach this issue in the same way as any other material. Working on the resistance is at least as important as the content of the secret. In other words, what is it in the patient that has required the secret to be hidden? This point is summed up by the adage, "Never rape the patient for the secret."

• *Ego before id* is a similar technical rule. The ego is that part of the personality that perceives and thinks. The id contains the drives, impulses, and desires.

As an illustration, if a therapist perceived that a man was struggling with unconscious homosexual feelings, one approach would be to ask her patient how he might feel if he discovered homosexual feelings within himself. This is the ego's domain (thinking and reacting). Only afterward might she directly interpret his homosexual longings (id impulses).

Similarly, a therapist might focus on a patient's reactions to his angry feelings, for example, fear or self-criticism (ego attitudes), before emphasizing the white-hot anger itself (an id impulse).

This discussion of the functions of the ego and the id is necessarily abbreviated. For example, the ego also tries to conform to the values of the superego, which judges and punishes with feelings of guilt or shame. The purpose of introducing these concepts here is solely to provide an introduction to how to proceed with a patient. For more information on the structural theory (id, ego, superego), I recommend Brenner's (1955) *An Elementary Textbook of Psychoanalysis*.

Begin at the surface is one of the most helpful rules. In the approach to interviewing described in Chapter 2 we emphasized listening to whatever the patient chooses to speak about. This constitutes the surface. Wherever the discussion goes, it should follow from this opening.

The "oversexed" male patient mentioned earlier began by telling his therapist about his numerous sexual conquests, how much he enjoyed sex, and so on. Gradually, the loneliness associated with multiple short relationships surfaced. Only after that could his anxiety about emotional closeness and his fear of being abandoned come into focus. At each step, his therapist was able to stay with the current surface, only deepening the therapy when the patient was ready.

A related maxim is, "The patient is always right." This means that however a patient describes his world, he is speaking the truth as he experiences it.

An inexperienced therapist told a paranoid patient that he seemed to be angry. "No, I'm not angry!" the man retorted through clenched teeth. The live-wire tension in the patient was enough to make the therapist back off. However, the patient was right in the sense that he did not recognize that he harbored anger and rage within.

For purposes of therapy, even lies by the patient make relatively little difference to the process of the work (although they may irritate the therapist). If a patient lies, he feels, based on his life experience up to that point, that lying is the best strategy. Often he is afraid. Certainly he is demonstrating his modus operandi. If the therapist and patient can create conditions of safety, most patients will become progressively more truthful. Many therapists are surprised by the common experience of having a seemingly truthful patient confess to a lie after many months of therapy. Pervasive lying may be a sign of severe psychopathology.

THE FEAR OF REGRESSION

Patients become dependent on their therapists during therapy. This dependency state involves a *regression*, a retreat to an earlier stage of psychological development. The patient becomes more childlike in relation to the therapist.

A patient increasingly looked forward to his therapy sessions, and valued highly whatever the therapist said (like a small child with a beloved father).

Another patient constantly feared his therapist's criticism. He felt that whatever he did, his therapist undoubtedly could do it better (like a child who felt inadequate compared with an adult).

In insight therapy this regression is intended to be temporary. One of its purposes is to allow a safe exploration of the "inner child" within the patient. Furthermore, the regressed patient has temporarily loosened his fixed adjustment as an adult. Thus he can change his patterns more easily.

In this regression, a patient feels vulnerable. Fears of intimacy with the therapist are often linked to unconscious fears of exploitation and engulfment. Furthermore, a patient always has some resentment toward a therapist he feels dependent on. It is understandable that a person would resist putting himself in this position. It has been said that the first six months of any therapy is a defense against the regression.

In light of the above it is worthwhile for the therapist to help the patient articulate his fears about therapy.

> T: Since your previous relationships have not worked out very well, it's understandable that you might believe the same thing will happen here in your therapy.

It is not uncommon for some patients to have a "flight into health" after a few therapy sessions. Clinically, this has the appearance of a sudden improvement, accompanied by a decision to quit therapy. It is as if the patient has glimpsed the territory he would have to cross in therapy, and decided it was safer to stay home and make do.

If a patient is adamant about leaving, the therapist has little choice but to support the patient's decision. The best the therapist can do is to remind the patient that the door remains open should he wish to return. (See Chapter 16 for a further discussion of sudden terminations.)

In summary, Semrad's (Rako and Mazer 1980) advice to a therapist might especially apply to the opening phase:

> Don't get set on curing her, but on understanding her. If you understand, and she understands what you understand, then cure will follow naturally. [p. 122]

CHAPTER 10

Some Technical and Boundary Issues

- Therapy with family members or friends
- Notes and tape recording
- Length and frequency of sessions
- Lateness and missed appointments
- Telephone calls
- When to refer for medication evaluation
- Gifts
- Confidentiality
- Touching
- Contact after therapy

Boundaries in psychotherapy refer to the appropriate limits of the interaction between patient and therapist. At times patients may invite boundary violations, which would be immediately gratifying to both parties. Ultimately, however, the results would be confusing and damaging to the patient. A therapist having sex with a patient is a primary example. The therapist is responsible for maintaining boundaries. (The concept of the boundary is related to the *frame*, discussed in Chapter 8.)

Boundary dilemmas constitute some of the most difficult problems in insight psychotherapy. The following issues relate both to boundary problems and general issues of technique.

THERAPY WITH FAMILY MEMBERS OR FRIENDS

It is both impractical and unethical to attempt formal psychotherapy with friends or family members. The dual relationship of friend and therapist interferes with the formation and understanding of transference. The therapist is compromised by conflicting interests and cannot be objective. For good reason, experienced therapists usually shy away from treating even casual acquaintances.

THERAPY WITH FAMILY MEMBERS OR FRIENDS OF PATIENTS

It is often gratifying for a therapist to be referred a family member or a friend of a current patient. Unfortunately, accepting such referrals is fraught with difficulty. Problems exist especially in the areas of conflict of interest and confidentiality.

A therapist treating a husband and wife separately might encounter the following dilemma: The wife tells the therapist in confidence that she is having an affair. She does not want her husband to know. In his session, the husband tells the therapist that he had a dream in which his wife was having an affair. How free can the therapist be to work with the man and his dream?

In this situation, each patient (spouse) may attempt to use the therapist to deliver messages. And the temptation for both patients to see the therapist as a judge (parent) will be intense.

When a therapist sees a child and a parent separately, it is extremely difficult (usually for the child) to believe that the therapist maintains confidentiality. Furthermore, there will be continual testing of the therapist.

A 13-year-old girl told her therapist that she was sexually active, and that her mother was secretly an alcoholic. The mother, who was seeing the same therapist, was strictly religious, with nearly delusional fears of her daughter getting pregnant or contracting AIDS. The therapist's attempts to see them together were largely unsuccessful, resulting either in screaming matches or canceled appointments. This situation sputtered along for more than a year without either patient developing a good working relationship with the therapist.

These same problems, in various forms, apply to treating two close friends. Although it is better if the therapist can avoid these situations, there are exceptions based on unusual circumstances. These are best discussed with an experienced supervisor.

The problems discussed above usually apply to former patients as well. Not treating a close relative or friend of a former patient protects the patient's option to return for more help at some future time.

It is also worth remarking that these views represent only this author's opinion. Some insight therapists feel that treating family members separately is workable. This discussion also should not be interpreted as critical of marital or family therapy. These approaches can be extremely powerful. Learning these approaches can be as demanding and time-consuming as learning psychoanalytic psychotherapy (Haley 1970).

FIRST NAMES?

How should a therapist address a patient? Last names may be too formal, and first names may be too familiar. Some therapists avoid the issue by trying not to call the patient by any name. Similarly, does the therapist identify himself as "Doctor," "Mister," or "Bob?" Again, many therapists partially avoid the issue by using both names:

> T: Hello. I'm Robert Wilson, and you must be Julie Matthews.

Some therapists ask the patient what she prefers to be called. In turn, this may prompt the patient to ask the therapist how she should address him.

If the forms of address are symmetrical (both therapist and patient use either first or last names), a sense of equality is promoted in the relationship. The patient is more likely to see the therapist as "on the same level." Conversely, if the therapist is "Mr. Wilson" while the patient is "Julie," a status difference is acknowledged, with the patient at a disadvantage.

Nevertheless, a patient who calls her therapist "Mr. Wilson" may not be affected adversely in any way. Both patient and therapist have comfort levels with forms of address based on cultural and personal sensitivities. The therapist should be guided by what he and the patient feel most comfortable with. If the issue comes up for discussion, the therapist might state his preference:

> T: I'm more comfortable if we both use either first or last names, because it implies a sense of equality.

Or,

> T: I call you Ms. Matthews out of respect. You may call me whatever is comfortable for you.

Or the therapist may choose to explore the issue:

> T: How would it feel for you to call me by my first or my last name?

NOTES

Most therapists make notes of some kind, usually after the sessions. Writing in the patient's presence may interfere with spontaneity and be distracting. The purpose of notes is to help the therapist do the work, and this should be the guiding principle. Practice in this area varies widely. Some therapists do not keep any notes. In many states patients have a right to see their records upon request. There may also be some legal implications, especially if the therapist is later accused of malpractice.

The situation is more complex if the therapist works for a clinic. In this situation, some idea of the issues the patient is working on should be recorded, though a therapist might well choose to leave out some sensitive details, to protect the patient's privacy.

TAPE RECORDING

Sometimes patients will ask to tape-record their sessions. This is a sensitive area and ideally should be discussed openly. A tape of the session can be both reassuring for the patient (providing a feeling of safety if she is frightened), and useful, if she listens to it afterward.

Tape recordings can also have negative effects. Either the therapist or the patient may feel inhibited, knowing that every spoken word is preserved. The patient might also feel that she has magically "captured" the therapist, diverting focus away from the actual interaction (although this itself could be explored in the sessions).

If the therapist wishes to tape the sessions for use in supervision or for his own review, he should explain this to the patient and be guided by her response. It is both unwise and unethical to tape-record without the patient's knowledge.

FREQUENCY OF SESSIONS

This is an important issue. Many therapists assume that sessions once a week are usual, and do not even attempt to see patients more frequently. If a patient is suitable for insight therapy, twice a week sessions often produce more than twice the progress of once a week (assuming that such quantifications were actually possible).

More frequent sessions generally make therapy deeper and more intense. Transference, regression, and emotional involvement are increased. Working twice a week enables both therapist and patient to continue the process more easily, and less time is devoted simply to keeping up with external events.

In certain patients, insight therapy will generate intense feelings that will require meetings more often than once a week. Examples include acute grief and the sequelae of severe psychological trauma. The therapist can provide more support for these feelings by seeing the patient more often. The patient will feel safer knowing she will have another therapy session in three or four days, rather than in a week.

With obsessive-compulsive patients, meeting twice weekly enables the therapist and patient to engage more effectively. Because of their rigid defenses, these people are easier to work with if seen more often than once a week.

On the other hand, twice weekly meetings make the therapeutic relationship more intense. The heat can be hard to handle. The technical challenges are likely to be more difficult (for example, stronger positive or negative transference reactions). For an inexperienced therapist, ongoing supervision is especially important when the patient is seen more frequently than once a week (see Chapter 17).

Experienced therapists disagree on how necessary it is to see patients more often than once a week. Most believe that more can be accomplished with two or more sessions per week. A minority holds that people may only be able to change so fast, regardless of how frequently they see their therapists. Obviously, this may vary with different individual patients and therapists. The number of meetings per week can also be variable, with more frequent meetings occurring at times of crisis.

Inexperienced therapists are often reluctant to suggest twice weekly meetings to their patients, especially at the beginning of treatment. Given this tendency, I would encourage beginning therapists, if in doubt, to try to see some of their patients more often than once a week.

> T: I think our work would go faster if we met twice a week.
>
> P: Do you think I'm that sick?
>
> T: Actually, it's because I think you have the strength to work in that way. I think you'll find it more helpful. But if we do it, it's only a trial period to find the best way to work together.

Even if a patient cannot arrange to come more often than once a week, it is important for the therapist to give his opinion, if it can be done without scaring the patient.

> T: I understand that because of your financial situation you can't come here more often than once a week. In the future, things might change. At that point, it might be useful to consider coming more often.

Sometimes the right rhythm of sessions is only obtained after several trial periods.

Sessions every other week are less likely to produce a useful ongoing therapeutic process. They can be tried if that is the only possibility.

LENGTH OF SESSIONS

Freud saw his patients for 60-minute sessions. For many years, 50 minutes was standard. More recently, 45 minutes has become customary. Shorter sessions are sometimes used for supportive psychotherapy, but less than 45 minutes is likely to make insight therapy more difficult. Some patients request longer sessions, or double sessions, and, if the therapist feels comfortable, these may work out for the best. There is no certain best length for sessions.

THE THERAPIST IS THE TIMEKEEPER

It is important for the therapist to start and end the sessions on time. There are many advantages to this, including convenience for the therapist's own schedule. For the patient, one advantage is that the therapist's promptness conveys mutual respect and models committed, predictable, grown-up behavior for the patient (the therapist does what he says he is going to do).

A more subtle situation occurs when a therapist allows the patient extra time because of what she brings up near the end of a session. If, for example, she is about to reveal a secret and the therapist allows her extra time, he is saying, in effect, "If you talk about things that interest me enough, I will extend the session." How will the patient react in the next session, if she feels she has brought up something especially important, but the therapist ends the session on time? Furthermore, the patient may tailor her presentations in order to save dramatic details until the end, in order to get extra time.

It is also possible that a patient may feel one down and indebted to the therapist if he goes over time.

A therapist at a low-cost clinic went fifteen minutes over twice in a row with a patient. In the next session the patient said, "We'll stop a half hour early today, and I'll pay you the same amount, so we'll be even."

If a therapist consistently maintains the time boundary, the patient learns to rely on this. She may wait until the end of a session to mention something that she is not yet ready to discuss at length. This is her way of safely introducing the subject. If the therapist were to extend the hour, she would lose that advantage.

Although there are exceptions, beginning therapists should try to end sessions on time if possible. If a patient is preoccupied with time (watches the clock), or suggests that the time is up early, the therapist can point out:

> T: You don't have to worry about the time if you don't want to. I'll keep track of it.

If a patient has trouble leaving, the therapist can give the patient some warning.

> T: I can see that you're in the middle of something important [or upsetting]. We still have a few minutes, but I wanted to let you know we're going to have to stop soon.

Sometimes the therapist will have difficulty interrupting a garrulous patient. The problem is that some patients will go on and on, seemingly without even taking a breath, while the therapist becomes more and more fidgety.

> T: I can see that you're in the middle of this discussion, but we will have to stop for today.

Or,

> T: I'm sorry to be interrupting you, but we can start in the same place next time if you like.

In these situations, ending on time is important because by doing so the therapist symbolically represents reality, with its boundaries and limitations.

If a therapist repeatedly has to interrupt a patient in order to end the sessions, that should be discussed during a subsequent session.

> T: How do you experience the endings of our sessions? (pause for the patient's response) I wonder if you feel interrupted or cut off by me. (Pause) If so, how do you feel about that?

An unavoidable exception to ending on time occurs when a patient becomes upset at the very end of a session. Here a therapist could say:

> T: We're going to have to stop for today, but why don't you take a few minutes and collect yourself before you leave.

If this phenomenon begins to become a pattern, it could be dealt with later on.

LATENESS

If a patient is late, in general, therapists need not make up the time, though some do if they have the time and the lateness is infrequent.

Sometimes it is useful to inquire about the meaning of lateness, especially if it is a pattern.

> T: What occurs to you about being late?
>
> P: Things were really hectic at work and I just got behind. (In this situation, the therapist probably should not pursue the matter.)

However, the patient may be ready to address the issue:

> T: What occurs to you about being late?
>
> P: Maybe I really didn't want to come.
>
> T: Tell me more about that.

If in doubt about whether or not to confront the patient, it is better to wait. This is because it is likely that the patient will feel criticized. Patients often fear that the therapist is angry at them for being late, rather than that he is trying to understand.

Although lateness can be symbolic of many things (fear of dependency, hostility, etc.), sometimes a patient will maintain this pattern for a long period of time in spite of considerable discussion. At all events, it is best to avoid badgering the patient.

If the therapist is late, he should apologize sometime during the hour, and make up the extra time at the end of that hour, or, if that is not possible because of his or the patient's schedule, in a subsequent hour. Making up the time in a future hour may have primarily symbolic value, but nevertheless can be important. If asked why he was late, the therapist might answer directly or ask the patient:

> T: What thoughts [or fantasies] do you have about that?
>
> P: Maybe you had an emergency.
>
> T: How would you feel if that were true?
>
> P: I could understand that. Those things happen. I hope that the person is all right.
>
> T: What other thoughts do you have?
>
> P: Maybe you wanted to finish having lunch with your wife.
>
> T: How would you feel about that?

P: I wouldn't like it.

T: Yes, I'd be putting my convenience ahead of your appointment.

MISSED APPOINTMENTS

If a patient misses an appointment without calling, I recommend calling the patient during the hour. Not all therapists agree with this, and many wait until the patient calls them. One reason for calling during the hour is that it emphasizes that the time really belongs to the patient. Furthermore, although the patient may have forgotten the hour, she may also have been in an accident or had some other mishap, and the therapist's calling is simply human. Finally, calling at the time prevents the therapist from having such a long list of calls to make at the end of the day.

Most patients expect to be charged for failed appointments. In addition to trying to understand the patient's experience, the therapist can ask:

T: What are your thoughts about the fee for the missed hour?

P: Well, of course I have to pay you.

Or:

P: What is your policy?

T: Ordinarily, I charge for missed appointments. How does that policy seem to you?

P: Well, I guess I can understand it.

If a patient calls more than 24 hours in advance to cancel an appointment, most therapists do not charge. The best policy is to try to reschedule the appointment. Some therapists try to assess the reasons for the cancellation before deciding whether or not to charge. For example, if a patient has a flat tire on the way to the appointment, or a mother must stay home with a sick child, many therapists do not charge. Regardless of his policy, the therapist should discuss the matter with the patient, and honor her reaction. Sometimes splitting the fee feels like a fair and acceptable solution.

There is a long history of discussion about charging for missed hours. Freud recommended, "leasing by the hour," but he saw his patient at a set hour, six days a week. Some of his patients even accompanied him on vacations! Some therapists try to charge for all missed hours, regardless of the reason. Others charge if they cannot fill the patient's hours with other patients. The 24-hour rule has gained wide acceptance in some areas, but there is a case to be made for assessing each situation individually.

Although there are exceptions, if a patient calls to cancel a session on short notice, it is usually best if the therapist does not try to talk the patient into coming on the telephone. It rarely works, and the patient frequently feels pressured or devalued.

It is a different matter if a patient calls and announces on the telephone that she is quitting. Then it is very important for the therapist to try to arrange at least one "wrap-up" session (see Chapter 16).

THERAPIST ABSENCES

Generally, it is best to give the patient as much notice as possible about therapist absences, vacations, and so on. It is usually preferable to tell the patient,

> T: I will be away from August first to August fifteenth.

rather than

> T: I will be on vacation from . . .

The reasons for this include (1) allowing for the patient's fantasies, and (2) the therapist may not want to tell the patient he is having a hemorrhoidectomy or has to go to his child's school for a disciplinary conference.

Sudden absences of the therapist are not easy to deal with. Sometimes it is best to share the reason with the patient. In the case of illness of the therapist or a family emergency, care must be taken that the patient feels she can still rely on the therapist, once he is back at work. This is conveyed mostly by the attitude of the therapist, as well as in discussions:

P: I was sorry to hear of your mother's death.

T: Thank you for your sympathy. (Pause) Perhaps now you wonder if I'm okay and we can get back to work.

TELEPHONE CALLS

Most psychotherapy patients never call their therapists except to change appointments. More disturbed patients who are often in crisis are more likely to call their therapists. Some therapists have greater tolerance for after-hours phone calls than others, and some therapists get considerably more calls than others.

Although many therapists now carry pagers, except when working with hospitalized or suicidal patients (see Chapter 15), I do not believe therapists should have to do this. In reality there are very few true psychological emergencies—situations that involve life or death, or where delay will cause serious harm to a patient.

On the other hand, I believe therapists should *always* return phone calls from patients. I also believe that trying to do therapy on the telephone, especially on demand, is not a good idea. If the therapist has time to talk, the patient may consider it her due, and then be additionally upset if, on another occasion, the therapist does not have time. Lengthy phone conversations confirm the dramatic idea that a problem must be dealt with *right now* and cannot wait. Charging for phone calls also conveys the idea that such calls are legitimate and proper.

If a patient calls in crisis, naturally the therapist must try to help. Scheduling an extra session as soon as possible is often the most helpful response. The therapist must try to steer a course between trying to help and understand, and limiting the extent of the call. When patients are upset, reassurance that the therapist is interested and reliable is often helpful. One way of conveying this to an anxious patient is to suggest that the patient call the therapist back at a certain time a few hours later.

> T: I don't think we are going to be able to help you solve this problem completely on the phone. Obviously you are very upset. Why don't you call me this evening at 9 P.M. and let me know how you are doing.

There are a variety of techniques for dealing with patients in crisis on the phone, depending on whether the crisis is a panic attack, fears of harming someone, or a suicidal crisis. Often the patient will suggest something helpful if asked.

> T: What do you think you could do to help yourself right now?
>
> P: Well, I could call my friend and talk to her
>
> [or: go for a walk, clean the house, write in my journal, take one of my tranquilizers].

These are also recommendations a therapist might make. Niceties of trying not to make suggestions often fall by the wayside after midnight.

The goal is to try to tide the patient over until the issues can be dealt with in the therapy hours. A general principle is, Always discuss the phone call and its context in a subsequent therapy hour. The therapist and the patient need to know how the crisis developed and how the patient might deal with a similar situation the next time it occurs. This is important because behavior that results in gratification from the therapist outside of the therapy hour and is not dealt with is likely to recur.

If a therapist feels that some contact with the patient between sessions is necessary for support, it is best to schedule brief calls at a mutually convenient time. The therapist can explain that these calls are not sessions, but only touching base to help the patient stabilize herself during a crisis.

If possible, it is better to have the patient call the therapist, because it gives the patient the responsibility and a more active role. However, if the patient fails to call at the appointed time, the therapist should call. Again, the patient's experience of this phone contact should be discussed in the next face-to-face meeting.

If the therapist is not comfortable with these types of arrangements, he should not volunteer, but simply tell the patient that if she does not know what to do during a crisis, she can go to a hospital emergency room (or call a hotline, if one is available).

WHAT IF THE PATIENT IS DRUNK?

If a patient arrives at a session drunk or under the influence of drugs, the therapist finds himself in a difficult position. One alternative is to tell the patient,

> T: We need to have all of you here, not with part of your mind anesthetized with alcohol [or altered by drugs]. Let's plan on meeting next week at our regular time, drug free.

If the patient is not too far gone, the therapist can go ahead and try to work with her, but with the knowledge that the session may do little good. At some point without "beating up the patient," the therapist should emphasize how important it is for the patient to come to the sessions clean. (Some therapists would disagree with this approach, and would never work with a patient who was under the influence of drugs.)

One variant of this problem includes an opening such as:

P: I took a Valium before I came today.

Here the therapist can work with the patient to understand what was going on before she took the pill, as well as what effects she feels from having taken it. He can also urge her to try to come to future sessions without taking a tranquilizer.

If a patient is intoxicated, the therapist has a responsibility to see that she has a safe way to get home. He would then need to deal with this event in future sessions.

WHEN TO REFER FOR MEDICATION EVALUATION

Psychiatrists can prescribe medications for their own patients. All other mental health professionals need to refer their patients to physicians (usually psychiatrists) for medications.[1] When is such a referral appropriate?

Medications are most useful in *depression*, *psychosis*, and *anxiety*, especially panic attacks. A few other conditions,

---

[1]One exception is that psychiatric nurse practitioners can obtain "furnishing" licenses in most states, enabling them to prescribe some medications. This section will be addressed primarily to nonmedical therapists, although the principles for deciding when to seek a medication evaluation and when to consider prescribing medications are similar.

such as attention deficit disorder and severe obsessive-compulsive disorder, are sometimes treated successfully with medications.

Depression

The more severe the depression, the more likely antidepressants will be helpful. In addition to severity, the following factors predispose to a successful response to medication:

1. Biological or vegetative (autonomic nervous system) signs
   a. sleep disturbance (insomnia or hypersomnia)
   b. change in appetite (decrease or increase, especially if there has been a loss or gain in weight)
   c. decreased sex drive
   d. decreased energy and activity
   e. symptoms worse in the morning
2. Recent onset of symptoms
3. "Biological feel"—a characteristic hard to define, but such patients seem to be psychologically opaque and often are not intellectually curious or introspective.

In spite of these predictors, it is impossible to tell in advance which patients will benefit from antidepressants. Some severely depressed patients do not respond, and some patients with mild depression or different psychiatric symptoms obtain great benefit from antidepressants. For these reasons it is sometimes very difficult to tell which patients should have a trial of antidepressant medication. Other factors than the degree of disturbance, such as patient and therapist preferences, often strongly influence the decision.

When in doubt, a nonmedical psychotherapist might be advised to suggest a medication evaluation. Even if they are initially reluctant, many patients eventually appreciate a "no stone unturned" approach. Furthermore, requesting an evaluation is not necessarily a decision for medication. I believe trainees and therapists from all disciplines should feel free to call their medical consultants and discuss their patients at any time. Continued contact over time between a patient's therapist and a prescribing physician is clearly in the patient's interest.

An additional factor in favor of medication is the safety of modern psychopharmacologic agents. The risk of permanent harm from properly prescribed antidepressants is minuscule.

It used to be thought that prescribing antidepressants or other medications would hinder psychotherapy, by decreasing the patient's pain and therefore motivation for change. In practice, this is rarely observed. Generally the opposite reaction occurs: a patient who has responded to medication generally works better in therapy! Depressed patients, for example, have more energy for the work.

Here is an example of how a therapist might suggest a medication evaluation:

> T: Your feelings of depression sound really painful. There has been a lot of publicity about medications for depression. What thoughts have you had about taking them?

Depending on the patient's response, the therapist might then add:

> T: It's well known that many depressions have partly biological causes. I think it would be worthwhile for you to see a psychiatrist for an evaluation for antidepressant medications. Of course, we will keep working on what's going on, but this will give you every advantage. How does this strike you? (pause) I usually work with Dr. Johnson and here is his phone number.

It is important for the therapist to emphasize continuation of the psychotherapy. Many patients feel that the therapist is suggesting medications for one of the following reasons:

1. The therapist feels like giving up.
2. The patient is too difficult.
3. The therapist does not know what else to do.
4. The therapist would like to get rid of the patient.

Patients may spontaneously voice these fears:

> P: Are you recommending medications because you don't think you can help me?

> T: That sounds like a really scary thought. Maybe it sounds like I'm giving up on you.

Or the therapist might raise these issues:

> T: I feel like I'm in a dilemma. Sometimes patients feel that therapists suggest medications to get rid of them or to shut them up. On the other hand, if medications would help, even a little, then my not bringing them up isn't good either.

> P: Medications are just a crutch and I don't want to take them.

> T: Tell me more about what you mean.

Feelings of shame and weakness may be revealed in the ensuing discussion.

It is important to support a patient's decision not to try medications.

> T: I'm comfortable working with you, with or without medications. If at some point in the future you would like to reconsider, you can let me know.

Psychosis

Psychotic patients frequently improve with medications. Schizophrenics usually benefit from neuroleptics (formerly called major tranquilizers or antipsychotics). However, the more chronic the condition, the less likely medications are to be helpful. A patient with a long-standing, fixed delusional system is especially unlikely to respond to neuroleptics.

Manic and depressive psychoses often respond to specific pharmacologic agents.

Anxiety

Panic attacks, often characterized by fears of dying, are extremely frightening to patients. These are frequently responsive to some antidepressants.

Other forms of anxiety are often treated by benzodiazepine drugs such as Valium, Ativan, and Xanax. These drugs have an addiction liability and are frequently overused. Furthermore, they rarely promote the process of growth. However, in some cases they have value when used intermittently. Being able to take a pill when very anxious helps to give a patient a sense of control. There can also be a soothing, transference meaning to putting something inside that was authorized (fed) by the patient's therapist. (In other individuals' minds, the medications can also be seen as poison.)

If antianxiety drugs are prescribed, it is useful for the therapist to ask the patient to keep her informed of how and when he uses them. This approach helps bring the patient's experience of anxiety into the therapy, and it helps the therapist keep track of the possibility of addiction.

Other Conditions

Attention deficit disorder and severe obsessive-compulsive symptoms are sometimes responsive to medications, as are rarer conditions, such as Tourette's Disorder (consisting of motor and vocal tics) and narcolepsy (characterized by suddenly falling asleep).

Patients with borderline personality disorder (used here in a broader sense than in *DSM-IV*) unfortunately are not regularly helped by medications.

GIFTS

If a patient brings a gift to his therapist, she should ordinarily accept it. Accepting the gift is a human response, and if the therapist were to reject the gift, it would be a demeaning and hurtful experience for the patient. The meaning of the gift to the patient should then be explored, through inquiries about the patient's fantasies, if necessary.

T: What fantasies did you have about my wearing this scarf?

The relationship context is also important. Sometimes a gift is an expression of love or gratitude, or it may be a propitiatory offering to ward off hostility.

An exception to the policy of accepting all gifts is a very large or expensive present. However, the traditional position in psychoanalysis has been to analyze the meaning of gifts before they are accepted by the therapist, so some supervisors might disagree with my position.

CONFIDENTIALITY

With adults, many therapists do not introduce the subject of confidentiality until the patient does. Then, of course, the therapist can confirm nearly absolute confidentiality. Other therapists, especially in clinic settings, prefer to discuss the subject in an early meeting, emphasizing the legal limitations. This is the usual practice with children and adolescents.

The exceptions to complete confidentiality relate to the laws of the state or country in which the therapist practices, and perhaps certain higher moral principles. One example of these latter might be informing a patient's family if suicide is a risk.

For the most part, the laws relating to confidentiality are generally reasonable, and are aimed at preventing harm to others or the patient. For example, the requirement to report child or elder abuse takes the decision out of the therapist's hands. When he has to make such a report, the therapist can straightforwardly explain the law and his decision. Then he can accept and discuss the patient's response.

The duty to warn of impending violence is usually consistent with good clinical practice. If a therapist seriously believes a patient is likely to harm someone, any reasonable therapist would do anything he could to prevent it. This would also be in the patient's interest, and could be explained in that way to the patient.

Telephone calls to the therapist about the patient from family members or others are fairly common events. I believe it is only courteous to return all phone calls. The therapist can explain to the caller that he cannot even acknowledge who his patients are, let alone divulge any information. On the other hand, the therapist will tell the caller that his policy is to tell his patients everything he hears said concerning them. Sometimes it is important to try to say this to the caller early in the conversation, before the caller divulges more than he or she wants to. Sometimes it is necessary to be quite firm:

> T: I don't wish to be rude, but I really can't say anything about any of my patients or even acknowledge who they are. I'm sure you can understand why this is important for the therapeutic relationship. I returned your call as a courtesy, but I don't think I can be of further help to you directly. I also don't think it's good for me to deliver messages to my patients.

This last refers to the therapist's dilemma when a spouse, or sometimes an ex-spouse, of a patient calls the therapist and insists on complaining about the patient to the therapist.

Sometimes it is possible to say to a distraught family member:

> T: I can tell you a general principle—namely that openness and honesty are frequently the best policies. People need to be straight with each other in order to work things out.

Calls from another therapist, for example, one who is seeing the patient's spouse or child, need to be considered on an individual basis. If the therapist wishes to talk about the patient in these instances, he needs to have the patient's permission. Sometimes a therapist would prefer not to discuss his patient with the therapist of a family member, because he wishes to use only data he has gathered directly from the patient. As soon as he has begun to receive information from someone else about his patient, the therapist's perspective is subtly changed. The wishes of individual therapists in these situations should be respected.

In some situations information obtained from friends of the patient or other therapists can be destructive:

> Friend of patient: Did you know your patient was fired yesterday?

Or:

> Wife (also a therapist) of patient's therapist: My patient suspects that your patient is having an affair.

TOUCHING

In psychoanalytic psychotherapy touching a patient generally creates problems. A major thrust of the method is to help a patient master herself through insight. Putting it into words helps a person control her impulses and allows both patient and therapist to look at what they mean.

P: I'm really frightened. Would you hold my hand?

T: I can see that you are upset, and I'd like to help you. The way I feel I can do that best is if you can put your fears into words, and I will respond. What are you frightened of? (Later) How would it feel if I were to hold your hand? (Still later) How did you react to my not taking your hand?

Or:

T: I am holding your hand through our psychological work together.

The problem with touching is that it often leads to a confusion of boundaries in a borderline patient. Holding hands may be followed by a request for a hug. A short hug becomes a long embrace. At any point the patient may misinterpret the therapist's intentions. Nonverbal communications are generally open to wider inferences than are words.

A harmless exception to the general prohibition against touching is shaking hands with a patient after (and sometimes before) a session. This custom is best initiated by the patient, however. There are a few other clear exceptions, for example, congratulating a patient with a handshake upon an achievement such as a school graduation, a marriage, the birth of a child, or ending therapy.

The issue of touching is very difficult. There are schools of psychotherapy that acknowledge roots in psychoanalysis, such a bioenergetics, that routinely include physical contact. There are anecdotal accounts of good outcomes where therapists have touched their patients. Nevertheless, although this prescription is perhaps overly rigid, therapists are best off following Semrad's advice, "When you touch the patient, therapy is over" (quoted in Gutheil 1989).

CONTACT AFTER THERAPY BETWEEN THE PATIENT AND THE THERAPIST

Patients understandably may look forward to seeing their therapists as friends after therapy is over. First, they may genuinely like the therapist (and vice versa). Second, they may feel close to the therapist, who has understood and helped them, and not wish to experience the pain of loss. Third, the patient may unconsciously still feel a need to be supported by the therapist or to work on some unfinished issues.

Yet another powerful motive for seeing the therapist as a friend is to overcome lingering feelings of humiliation and feeling less than the therapist and others. A patient may anticipate a feeling of triumph when he reaches what feels like equal status. Finally, the patient may wish to repay the therapist, to give the benefits of friendship, such as help with family problems, gifts, and so on. Many other possible motives exist as well.

Contact with a patient after therapy is a difficult issue for the therapist. On the one hand, the therapist needs to protect the possibility of the patient returning for more therapy sometime in the future. On the other hand, the therapist wants to remain supportive and helpful to her former patients. She certainly does not want to rebuff or reject them. Furthermore, some social contact as equals may in fact help the patient work through issues of separation.

Close friendship between therapist and patient after therapy is almost never a good idea, since it would preclude the possibility of more therapy (with that therapist). It might also be difficult for both parties due to lingering unresolved transferences. When a sexual relationship is in question, it is worth remembering that some authors feel the parental transference of a former patient is never completely resolved: "Once a patient, always a patient." Following this line of reasoning, the Board of Trustees of the American Psychiatric Association voted in 1993 that sexual contact between a therapist and a former patient is always unethical. The vote was nine to seven, indicating that there was considerable controversy.

Casual contact between a patient and his former therapist may be unavoidable in some social settings. Many therapists will agree to limited social contacts with former patients. Examples might be going to lunch to catch up with events in the patient's life, attending a wedding, or occasionally chatting on the telephone.

If a patient writes to his former therapist, I recommend *always* answering. (I find it is best to do this immediately to avoid procrastination.) The answer need not be lengthy, but given the importance of the therapist for the patient, silence from the therapist will create a painful letdown.

CHAPTER 11

The Middle Phase of Psychotherapy

- Goals
- Interpretation
- Transference and countertransference
- Stalemates

GOALS

The goals of the middle phase are insight and behavior change. *Insight* is an increase in self-knowledge that leads to behavior change. *Behavior change*, in this sense, includes feelings and internal states of mind. For example, relief from feelings of anxiety or depression is a frequent goal of therapy. External behavioral goals range from being able to speak in public to creating an intimate relationship with the opposite sex.

The middle phase is the most variable and usually the longest phase of psychotherapy. To borrow an analogy from chess: The openings and endings follow certain principles that can be studied and taught. In the middle game there are fewer guidelines. This is where experience, intelligence, and creativity are most called upon.

Because the middle phase is the least predictable or orderly, a number of disconnected topics are covered in this chapter. They are all relevant to the exciting work that can occur in this phase.

When the middle phase is reached, the patient and therapist have learned something of how to work together. This phase is sometimes called the *working phase*. At least some of the time the patient and therapist share a mutual sense of purpose.

Paradoxically, in the middle phase the therapist may be confused, as the patient's transference distortions and emotional regression are at their height. Because of his identification with the patient, the therapist may be pulled into a patient's chaotic inner world, or he may be puzzled by the primitive affects and images the patient presents. Countertransference problems (involving the therapist's own issues) may also be the most pressing in this phase.

HOW TO LISTEN

Because of these cumulative pulls on the therapist, the traditional advice on how to listen to patients is especially valuable. Most therapists start out as good listeners for their friends. However, the way in which a therapist listens is different from having a heart-to-heart talk with a friend. The therapist listens in a deeper yet more fluid way, aimed at hearing the patient's unconscious. This may be learned only slowly (as it was in my own case).

Freud (1912b) recommended listening with "evenly suspended attention." "He [the analyst] should simply listen, and not bother about whether he is keeping anything in mind" (p. 112). In this way Freud felt the unconscious of the therapist would be most receptive to the unconscious of the patient.

Bion (1970) stated that the therapist should have "neither memory nor desire" when he or she listens to a patient. This is another way of describing the ideal receptivity of the therapist's mind. A well-known analyst likened the therapist's mode of being with a patient to listening to music. An experienced supervisor recommended that a therapist should start out trying to listen to patients with her heart rather than her head.

THE SHAPE OF A NEUROTIC PATIENT'S SESSION

Patients discuss material in three different arenas—the *present*, the *past*, and the *transference* (meaning the relationship with the therapist). Making connections between all three are essential in working, ongoing therapy.

When a neurotic (or high borderline) patient is working well in therapy, his sessions generally will have a specific "shape." He will start each session in the area of the transference. This may be only a discussion of the arrangements, such as confirming a future appointment time. It may be a comment about the therapist directly, or about her office. Or it may be a symbolic discussion of transference figures, such as another doctor, teachers, or political leaders.

Next, the patient will discuss issues in his present life, for example, his symptoms, his work, or his marriage. Then he will shift to the past, as he associates issues in the present with their precursors. Conflicts at work will remind him of conflicts with peers as a child, with teachers, or with his family. The recounting of these memories, when accompanied by affect, and together with understanding their connections to the present and the transference, constitute the heart of dynamic psychotherapy.

As the hour nears its end, the patient will return to

discussing issues in the present. Then, close to the end, the patient will spontaneously return to the relationship with the therapist (the transference).

Thus there is a sort of orderly mini-regression and return to the present in each hour.

If the patient is more borderline or psychotic, the session will not have this shape. Instead the areas the patient discusses will vary haphazardly. The patient may start with the present, then associate to the past, then to the transference, then back to the past, then to the transference again, then to the present, and so on. Although significant psychotherapeutic work can be done, the lack of structure of the sessions reflects the lack of coherence in the internal structure of the patient's mind. These two patterns are illustrated in Figure 11–1.

This dichotomy between a neurotic's and a borderline's session is highly schematic. Many sessions from both categories of patients do not follow these patterns. Nevertheless it is useful for a therapist to keep these patterns in mind, to train herself to listen for shifts of arena in the patient's material. These shifts can help organize the therapist's understanding of the hour. They can also serve as nodal points to help the therapist remember the sequence of the hour for review or for presentation to a supervisor.

MORE ON INTERPRETATION

Understanding the three arenas of patients' material leads to the maxim that a good interpretation can be likened to a three-ring circus. An ideal interpretation includes all three arenas: the transference, the present, and the past. In some cases the therapist may be able to say to the patient,

T: You are reacting to me with a sense of feeling belittled [the transference], just as you do with your boss

Figure 11–1. A Comparison of the Shape of a Neurotic versus a Borderline Patient's Hour

An example of a neurotic patient's hour

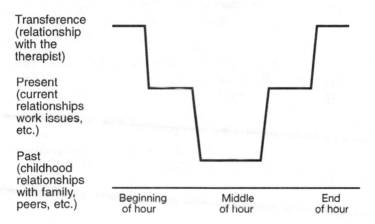

Transference
(relationship
with the
therapist)

Present
(current
relationships
work issues,
etc.)

Past
(childhood
relationships
with family,
peers, etc.)

Beginning   Middle   End
of hour   of hour   of hour

An example of a borderline patient's hour

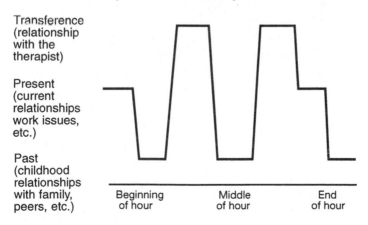

Transference
(relationship
with the
therapist)

Present
(current
relationships
work issues,
etc.)

Past
(childhood
relationships
with family,
peers, etc.)

Beginning   Middle   End
of hour   of hour   of hour

[the present], and just as you did with your father [the past].

Or:

> T: You idealized your father [the past] and each of your three husbands [the present]. Now it seems like you experience me in a similarly ideal way [the transference].

These complete interpretations may not occur very often. Greenson's four stages of interpretation—confrontation, clarification, interpretation, and working through (see Chapter 7)—imply that an interpretation in only one arena might develop slowly and by stages.

If a successful interpretation is made in one arena, it remains for the patient and the therapist to extend the insight into the other two arenas. For example:

> The assistant plant manager (see Chapters 6 and 7) at first recognized how angry he felt toward his boss who he felt belittled and exploited him (the present). In subsequent hours he began to realize that he had felt the same way with his father, who also had belittled him (the past).
>
> At about this time, the therapist happened to be five minutes late to a session, and had to cancel the next hour due to an emergency. The patient then complained about the therapist's "unreliability." Somewhat defensibly, the therapist pointed out that he had been punctual for many months. The patient then protested angrily that the therapist was belittling his complaint.
>
> It was only after the therapist acknowledged that he had reacted defensively that the patient could see that his own strong reaction (in the transference) was connected with his feelings toward his father and his boss, toward whom he had harbored angry feelings for years.

The process of interpretation in therapy is often gradual. Ideally, a patient should say "Yes" to every interpretation. This would indicate that each insight was just slightly beyond the patient's current knowledge of himself. In practice this seldom happens. Some interpretations are felt to be obvious or even redundant to a patient, while others are met with vehement denials.

If a patient says "No" to a therapist's interpretation, it is usually best for the therapist not to disagree. The patient has heard the therapist's comment, and it will remain in his unconscious. Furthermore, at times it is useful for the therapist to acknowledge that she can be wrong in her interpretations, to remind the patient that he is the final judge of what is true or not true about himself.

Even after an interpretation has been rejected, the therapist may make a similar comment if she hears the same theme in another hour. When the patient is ready to accept the insight, he may bring it up spontaneously, sometimes even as his own idea! (Naturally the therapist does not contradict him on this.)

Acceptance of interpretations comes in many forms. Freud commented that a patient saying, "I hadn't thought of that," is equivalent to "Yes."

Somewhat flippantly, it has been said that psychotherapy consists of telling people things they don't want to know about themselves. This is another way of stating the definition of interpretation: making the unconscious conscious. (In every instance, the patient has *repressed* the fantasy or feeling because he "didn't want to know.")

It is important to remember that psychotherapy deals with the recurrent themes in a person's life. Thus, a therapist need have little fear of missing something significant in any one hour, or even repeatedly. Precisely because his issues are the important themes in his life, the patient will always bring up significant issues over and over again (even if the therapist does not want to deal with them!).

Naturally, the therapist tries to understand the theme of each hour, and to make the sort of interpretation that one reads about (or hears from supervisors). However, knowing that there will be many opportunities to understand the patient helps a therapist to relax and be more available to understand the patient's world.

It has also been said that a patient can only absorb one interpretation per hour. On the one hand, each hour is a complete experience, with a beginning, a middle, and an end, while on the other hand, the beginning of each hour is a continuation from the end of the previous one, so that altogether they form an unbroken chain of experience. Thus, zero or three major interpretations might be useful in any one hour, since that hour is only a segment of the patient's continuous experience of therapy.

Further examples of interpretation are given below as part of the discussion of transference.

PROBLEMS RELATED TO NARCISSISM

The word *narcissism* means self-love. This concept is used in many different ways in the psychotherapeutic literature, sometimes referring to healthy self-esteem, sometimes to severe disturbances of a core sense of self.

This complex subject is relevant here in two significant ways. First, although a therapist may offer a brilliant interpretation to a patient, the patient may hear the therapist's comment as a criticism.

For example, the therapist *suggests*:

> T: You seem to react to me just as you did to your father.

while the patient *hears*:

> P: You react to me just as you did to your father, AND YOU SHOULDN'T!

If the therapist is sensitive to the patient's experience, she may recognize that this is happening:

> T: I'm wondering if you felt put down by my last comment.

A patient may also experience narcissistic injury (a blow to his self-esteem) when there has been an empathic failure or misattunement on the part of the therapist. For example:

> P: I will miss you next week when you are on vacation.
>
> T: Yes, and you would probably like me to have a rotten time.
>
> (Sorrowfully, the patient looked at the floor and said nothing for several minutes. Finally, with tears in her eyes, she responded:)
>
> P: I was only trying to tell you that I will miss you.

In this example, the therapist was trying to help the patient be aware of her anger at him for leaving her. However, his timing was off and the patient felt misunderstood and devalued.

Empathic failures on the part of the therapist occur in all therapies. Most are more subtle than the above example.

At a Monday morning session a patient began,

> P: I still didn't get the results.
>
> T: What were you expecting?
>
> P: The results of my pregnancy test last week. Did you forget? How could you!

A successful entrepreneur complained,

> P: Yesterday I lost three million dollars when Consolidated canceled our merger.
>
> T: Yes, but you still have more than ten million in the bank.

Sensitivity to the patient's experience and willingness to discuss these disruptions are essential to therapeutic progress. The subject of narcissism has received considerable attention in recent years, especially in the writings of Heinz Kohut (1977) and other self psychologists.

TRANSFERENCE—THE ENGINE OF CHANGE

The patient's experience of transference to the therapist is one of the most powerful forces contributing to growth and change. However, this is true only if the transference experience can be understood and used by the patient.

The therapeutic use of the transference has power because of the reality and immediacy of the patient's experience. When the assistant plant manager accused his therapist of belittling him, the patient felt his judgment to be entirely real. When the patient connected the similarity of this experience with how he had felt with his father, his anger at his therapist diminished, and that felt equally real.

It is a paradox that transference is both real and unreal at the same time, yet it feels entirely real to the patient. An example from everyday life is the idealization that accompanies falling in love, which usually contains unconscious transference elements.

But love is blind, and lovers cannot see
The pretty follies that themselves commit.
    (Shakespeare, *The Merchant of Venice*, Act II, Scene 6)

The mutual idealization of lovers may last a lifetime, or it may be eroded by the slow drip of reality. Sometimes the relationship develops violent swings from positive to negative, when lovers do not meet each other's idealistic expectations. When this happens, the unconscious hostility included in the transference aspect of the relationship begins to surface. This hostility is characteristic of transference reactions, which are by their nature essentially ambivalent, based on the ambivalence toward early parental figures (Freud 1912a, Greenson 1967). The schools of self psychology (Kohut 1977) and intersubjectivity (Stolorow and Atwood 1992) disagree with this view, contending that hostility is primarily a reaction to frustration and trauma. These theorists hold that transference does not always include unconscious hostility. They emphasize the positive, affirming aspects of the developmental bond of a child with its caregivers.

Clinically, transference reactions can be categorized in many ways. Most often they are divided into positive or negative, or toward mother or father. However, even these seemingly simple statements mask complexities. For example, there can be positive *and* negative feelings, toward both mother *and* father, based on experiences at different ages. Just as with disappointed or enraged lovers, transference reactions can change from one type to another very quickly.

All patients develop transference feelings toward their therapists, to some extent. For purposes of therapy, these feelings can be too strong, as sometimes happens with severely disturbed patients. In these cases, the patient may be overwhelmed with positive feelings, or may break off the treatment because of negative feelings. Other patients fail to develop enough transference involvement with their therapists, as is the case with some severe obsessive-compulsives or other isolated individuals.

Positive Transference

Positive transference is heir to all the loving and nurturing relationships that the patient has experienced in the past. It can induce a benign, positive atmosphere in therapy. When this is operative, the patient experiences the therapist as a loving and growth-enhancing parent. Positive transference may be relatively silent in the patient's material, or the patient may praise the therapist and describe feelings of longing to be with her.

In accord with the rule of interpreting transference only when it becomes a resistance (see below), many positive transferences should not be interpreted early in the course of therapy. However, if *idealization* of the therapist becomes too extreme, the therapist should attempt to deal with it. Ways to do this include pointing out its unrealistic nature (avoiding the temptation to attribute the patient's admiration simply to good judgment) and interpreting underlying hostility and envy (if the therapist perceives these).

An example of the problems associated with idealization occurred when a new patient announced,

> P: You are the only therapist in this whole city who I can work with. I've heard so many wonderful things about you. I'm sure that you can help me.

The experience of most therapists is that such a patient is unlikely to remain in treatment with anyone. The reason is that in all likelihood the patient has projected miraculous expectations onto his "fabulous" therapist. The patient in this example abruptly canceled his third appointment and did not return.

Self psychologists see idealization of the therapist as a narcissistic transference, based on a child's normal developmental need to idealize a parent (Kohut 1977). Therapists of this school generally do not confront idealization directly. Instead, they attempt to allow the idealization to diminish gradually. This occurs through unavoidable empathic failures on the part of the therapist. As these are processed, the patient gains a more realistic view of the therapist.

It is a cliché that patients fall in love with their therapists. *Erotized transferences* present special problems, especially if intense. When a patient begins to experience sexual feelings toward his or her therapist, it is important that these be addressed early. As with any other experience of the patient, the therapist must try to understand its meaning.

> T: You alluded to sexual feelings about me. What are these like?

If the patient can describe his or her desires, the work can go forward. Specific details of the fantasies are important. The patient's ideal may be blissful merger, similar to a mother and her nursing infant, or the patient may imagine being swept away and protected, as by a swashbuckling father. The goal here is to connect the patient's experience with the themes and continuity of his or her life.

There are many reasons why sexual feelings are difficult for therapists and patients. One aspect is addressed in the following:

> T: Perhaps you're worried that I'll get turned on by your telling me about your sexual feelings. On the one hand, I don't want to be intrusive. On the other, what does it say if we don't talk about them?

Patients often experience shame or embarrassment about sexual impulses toward the therapist.

> P: It's too embarrassing to talk about.
>
> T: Talking about it will help both of us learn more about what's going on with you, here and in your life outside of here. (Pause) How is it embarrassing?
>
> P: I'm sure you don't feel anything like that about me.

Here the patient is alluding to one aspect of erotized transferences. A patient may develop sexual feelings for the therapist in response to feeling devalued in other ways. It is as if the patient were saying, if you don't value and care for me, I will seduce you and then at least I will have something. This sexualization can be analogous to an infant who erotically self-stimulates when it has been neglected by its caregivers. Often the deeper wishes of patients are to be held and nurtured, rather than sexually fulfilled.

In addition to these two motives (hostility and wishes for nurturing), patients may develop sexual feelings for their therapists as replications of childhood experiences of overstimulation or overt sexual abuse.

Negative Transference

Negative transference feelings can vary from mild annoyance to intense, primitive rage. Negative transferences can be expected to occur in most insight therapies, sometimes for long periods of time. This is because most patients have had a considerable amount of negative experience with their parents (and other caregivers). These experiences are reawakened in the regression and dependency that develop in insight therapy. In fact, the more regressive the transference becomes, the greater will be the preponderance of hostile, aggressive strivings (Greenson 1967).

A second common source of negative transference relates to the expectations that patients bring to therapy. Almost always, patients hope for more than therapy realistically has to offer. Thus, some disappointment is inevitable and contributes to negative transference feelings. Some authors (Ursano et al. 1991) feel that disappointment is almost universal in the initial phase of therapy. They recommend that the therapist be alert to this issue, especially as it relates to negative transference. For example, the patient may feel that the therapist is not doing enough, or that the patient is being asked to do too much on his own, without sufficient support.

In Chapter 9 we discussed how it is a good sign whenever patients express feelings. This is especially true of the expression of negative feelings toward the therapist. Many inexperienced therapists feel defensive when attacked by their patients, and may fail to recognize the opportunity this presents.

In most patients' families of origin, the direct expression of negative feelings toward parents (and other caregivers) was not allowed. If such feelings were expressed by the child, the child was either punished or ignored.

When a patient expresses negative feelings toward the therapist directly, this can be a new and helpful experience. First, the therapist listens respectfully to the patient's feelings and complaints. Taking the patient seriously instead of responding defensively or punitively is helpful in itself. This attitude also shows the patient that the therapist is not destroyed by the patient's anger, which may be an unconscious fear.

Second, the therapist tries to work with the patient to understand the meaning of the patient's experience, which may include interpreting transference or projection. It may also include the therapist acknowledging errors and apologizing (see below).

When anger is expressed directly, and then processed by the patient and therapist, it demonstrates that the two can work things out, a valuable experience.

> T: So I have really disappointed you. And you are very angry at me—angry enough even to consider stopping therapy. However, rather than doing that, it is important to see if we can work this out. One of the reasons you came into treatment was that you were having trouble working things out in your relationships. This is like a

laboratory, and it may be very important for us to see this through. (Pause) What was the worst part of this for you?

In this example, the therapist used the word *anger*. For some patients this is a red-flag word, meaning unrestrained fury. For this reason, it is sometimes better to use words such as disappointment, annoyance, irritation, frustration, or resentment. If possible, it is best to use words that the patient uses. As the therapist and patient come to better mutual understanding, they will develop an accurate and mutually acceptable vocabulary.

The expression of negative transference should be welcomed by the therapist. Then these feelings (like any others) should be investigated.

> P: You are cold and aloof. No matter what I'm saying, you always stop on time. And even when I complain like this, you just listen and don't say anything. You're just like a machine.
>
> T: Not emotionally involved.
>
> P: Yes, just like my father!

The patient continued, vividly describing how she had felt neglected by her father.

Inexperienced therapists will sometimes get defensive, and respond as follows:

> T: I'm not cold. It's just that I have another appointment after yours.

This response ignores the transference. Furthermore, mentioning another appointment often feels demeaning to a patient, who may feel "put in his place."

A patient who is angry at her therapist finds herself in the following dilemma: If the therapist does not retaliate and responds only by trying to understand, he may appear aloof and loftily invulnerable to the patient's attack. As a result the patient feels impotent. On the other hand, if the therapist responds with anger, the patient may feel frightened and rejected. Furthermore, the patient may feel afraid to express herself freely in the future. There are times when all the therapist can do is to point out this paradox.

Negative transference is among the most difficult problems in psychotherapy. The ability of the therapist to work patiently at understanding it is all-important. Many therapists feel that if a patient does not get at her deep feelings of anger and rage, therapy is unlikely to have a lasting effect.

Referring to psychoanalysis (though I believe his comment applies equally to psychotherapy), Greenson (1967) wrote:

> In my experience and in the experience of others, the insufficiently analyzed negative transference is the most frequent cause of stalemated analysis. [p. 233]

Melanie Klein's (1957) theories particularly emphasize the role of the therapist as constantly dealing with patients' hatred.

WORKING WITH THE TRANSFERENCE

Beginning therapists often wonder how to recognize transference and when to interpret it. It is important to keep in mind that any person a patient mentions can be, in part, a symbolic representative of the therapist, especially if that person is an authority figure, such as a physician, priest, dentist, car mechanic (fixing the patient), or political leader.

All feelings a patient has toward the therapist contain transference elements, even though there may also be considerable reality in the patient's perception of the therapist.

A general rule is to interpret transference when it has become a problem for the therapy (when it has become a resistance). One sign of this is when the material has become repetitive. Another is when the transference threatens to become too great in either a positive or negative direction, exceeding an optimal level of intensity.

In the following examples, transference feelings were included in statements made directly to the therapist.

> P: You don't say anything to help me decide what to do.
>
> T: It sounds like you feel I'm letting you down.
>
> P: Yes, I need some help!

(Because this sequence had occurred in several previous hours, regarding an important decision that the patient faced in his work, the therapist felt that an interpretation might be helpful.)

> T: Maybe this feels like when you were growing up, when no one was available to help you.
>
> P: (Pause) Yes, it does.
>
> T: And at that time, you couldn't express how you felt. At least you're letting me know.
>
> P: Yes. I feel completely alone.
>
> T: I can see how painful this is for you. The decision you have to make is very difficult. It's understandable that you are struggling.
>
> P: Yes, it's really hard, and I'm scared I'll do the wrong thing.

This example illustrates a transference from two distant parents onto the therapist.

In the next example, the patient spoke positively about the therapist:

> P: It was really helpful last session when you said that I don't stick up for myself. You always know just the right thing to say.

T: (Having heard much praise over many hours from this patient) I appreciate your thanking me for my help. Sometimes, I bet I let you down too, though.

P: (Weakly) Not really . . .

T: It seems to me that you are reluctant to criticize me. Even when I'm running late and you have to wait. It seems like you act with me just like with your family, where everything always had to be nicey-nicey.

P: Well, you are late pretty often.

This transference reaction imbued the therapist with attitudes similar to how the patient's family had operated—don't complain or make waves.

At the beginnings of sessions patients often express transference feelings in disguised forms. Here are some examples:

P: What pretty flowers on your desk!

P: The magazines in your waiting room are always out of date.

P: The gas station across the street was closed again.

In each of these examples, the therapist did not respond at that moment, but chose to wait for more indications of a consistent theme.

Here are other examples of transference:

A patient complained that his child's teacher talked down to her students (just like he felt the therapist talked down to him).

Another patient complained at great length about the state governor who wanted to raise taxes, and, according to the patient, had no sympathy for low-income families. Later in the hour he spontaneously complained that the therapist's fee was too high.

A depressed man praised a quarterback who overcame numerous injuries and led his team to victory. When the therapist inquired if the patient feared that the therapist was injured or ill, the patient replied that he had noticed the therapist looking thin and worn out lately, and had been worried that he was ill. Significant in this patient's history was that he had cared for sick, elderly parents as a child. In the patient's transference reexperience, he feared the therapist was ill. His praise for the quarterback expressed the hope that the therapist would not succumb to illness, but would lead the patient to victory.

Recognizing clues to patients' unconscious transference with a "third ear" is a gradually acquired skill. Supervision can be very helpful.

A city dweller who learned to hunt squirrels in the backwoods needed the help of an experienced guide for many trips, before he could spot the squirrels for himself. At times even a sharp-eyed guide did not see a camouflaged squirrel.

PROLONGED TRANSFERENCE REACTIONS AND THE TRANSFERENCE NEUROSIS

It is especially important to be aware of prolonged transference reactions. These can represent a *transference neurosis*, in which the patient's core issues have come to be focused on the therapist. If understood, these developments offer the greatest opportunity for change.

The assistant plant manager who gradually became aware of his timid behavior and repressed hostility went through a long period of conflict with his therapist. At various times he felt his therapist belittled and demeaned him. Then, as the patient expressed his hostile feelings, he became afraid that his therapist would abandon him. In the next phase he became aware of deeply held wishes for nurturing and merger with his therapist. This in turn made him fearful of repressed homosexual wishes.

This series of regressive experiences (regressive because they reactivated passions and longings from earlier phases of his development) constituted a transference neurosis. The patient focused his core conflicts on the therapist. The interpretation of these led to an unshakable sense of conviction in the patient. As he worked through these issues he was able to integrate previously split-off aspects of himself, rendering him more whole, capable, and versatile.

The woman who had married three alcoholic men also developed a transference neurosis over the course of several years of therapy. Fairly early she developed sexual feelings for her sympathetic male therapist. Then, as these were not gratified in reality, she mobilized all of her feelings of abandonment and rage, focused on the therapist. There were many stormy sessions where she screamed at her therapist for being rejecting, cold, and uncaring.

As these feelings were worked through, and understood as replications of how she had felt toward both of her parents, she could accept the therapist's help, and began to make constructive changes in her life.

Prolonged transference reactions can be subtle and sometimes difficult to detect, because patients organize transferences around real characteristics of their therapists.

A therapist with formal manners was castigated by his patient for being aloof and distant. The patient had had distant parents. His transference feelings from the past fastened onto the social mannerisms of the therapist. What helped both the therapist, and eventually the patient, recognize that transference elements were involved was the inappropriate strength of the patient's feelings.

A patient asked her therapist for an extra session, which the therapist was unable to schedule. The patient became irate, accusing her therapist of not ever having cared about her. In time, it became clear that her feelings about her therapist overlapped with those toward her parents who, she felt, never had time for her. (She was one of twelve children.)

Clues to recognizing prolonged transference reactions include that these reactions are *inappropriate*, contain *strong affects*, or *resemble significant past relationships* in the patient's life.

The importance of the transference neurosis cannot be overemphasized. Because the patient comes to care passionately about issues in the therapy and about the therapist, insights achieved in this arena lead to a sense of conviction in the patient achievable in no other way.

Transference is one of the most interesting, difficult, and profound aspects of psychotherapy. Transference reactions are always mixed with other phenomena, such as projections, shifting identifications, and reality. For these reasons, regular supervision of new therapists' early cases is especially recommended.

Resolution of the transference often takes a considerable period of time. Multiple interpretations of each of its stages are usually necessary. Some aspects of the working-through process are not completed until long after therapy has ended (see Chapter 17).

THE WORKING ALLIANCE AND THE REAL
RELATIONSHIP

In addition to the transference, Greenson (1967) described two other aspects of the relationship between therapist and patient: the working alliance and the real relationship.

The *working alliance* refers to the rational, cooperative parts of the relationship between therapist and patient. It reflects their ability to work together (Greenson 1967). Because it is realistic, in a sense, it is the opposite of the transference. The working alliance permits the therapist and patient to observe the transference, and, for example, to agree that the patient (or sometimes the therapist) has misperceived or overreacted to present reality.

The therapist tries to foster the formation of a working alliance by inviting the patient to observe himself. She asks the rational part of him to confirm or deny her interpretive guesses. The therapist also tries to make the patient curious about himself, just as she is curious about him and his behavior. The goal is to learn to think about ourselves while in action.

The working alliance is confined to the therapeutic work that the therapist and patient do together. The *real relationship* (Greenson 1967) consists of aspects of the relationship between the two that are not transference and are not confined specifically to the work they do together. *Real* in this sense means not only realistic, but *genuine*.

The real relationship can include all the human interactions that take place between two people intimately involved in a serious project. Included in the real relationship are courtesies, reactions to errors, responses to significant events (inside and outside the treatment), and feelings of warmth and mutual regard that frequently develop as the therapeutic work proceeds.

In every psychotherapy, transference, the working alliance, and the real relationship overlap and interweave. The patient uses the working alliance in order to comprehend the therapist's point of view. However, transference can easily invade the working alliance. The therapist must continually keep the state of the working alliance in mind, and try to promote it whenever necessary. The real relationship is frequently implicit, but is continually important. It can manifest itself in reactions to real events such as expressions of joy at weddings or sympathy over losses.

A female college student discovered that her session took place on her therapist's birthday, because a bouquet was delivered to his waiting room. She was subdued during the early part of her session, but finally mentioned the flowers and their message. She felt resentful of his having received the gift and worried that he would be preoccupied with his celebration and not attentive to her.

The therapist commented that the situation seemed similar to how it was in her family, where her older brother was overtly favored by her parents. The patient fell silent for a moment, then roared, "Yes! You men get all the breaks. Everybody loves you, just because you're a man!" After a while she calmed down, but recounted many slights she had received compared with her brother.

As the session drew to a close, she apologized, saying, "I guess I overreacted. I hope you have a good birthday after all."

In this example, the patient's reaction to the therapist's receiving a gift on his birthday included significant transference elements from the patient's brother. When the patient was able to respond to the therapist's comment about her brother, and especially as she became more thoughtful, a good working alliance was present. At the close of the session, the patient's birthday wish for her therapist reflected the real relationship between the two.

COUNTERTRANSFERENCE

Earlier, we discussed the two meanings of countertransference. The narrower meaning denoted the therapist's transference to the patient. The broader meaning included all the feelings the therapist has in the presence of the patient or that relate to the patient.

The therapist's transference to the patient is, by definition in the narrow sense, a kind of unclarity. Perceptions and feelings from her own past may influence the therapist's experience of the patient. It is important that she try to be aware of her emotional reactions to her patients. Overreacting or feeling off balance may indicate countertransference, and can help alert a therapist to anxieties she might have in relation to the patient or his material.

A therapist whose sister was a lesbian had had considerable difficulty accepting her sister's identity. A patient of this therapist, a slightly younger professional woman, at first acted extremely competitive with her therapist. The therapist was able to deal effectively with this.

It was only when the patient began to express covert homosexual longings for the therapist that the therapist felt herself beginning to dislike the patient, being late for the patient's appointments, and so on. At this point the therapist sought supervision. It then became clear that the therapist was reacting negatively to the patient based on a reawakening of the turmoil that she had experienced with her sister. She was rejecting the patient just as she had wished to reject her sister.

Disliking the patient and being late for her sessions was how the therapist in this example experienced being off balance. Other ways can include feeling or doing something with particular patients that we do not ordinarily do.

All therapists have hidden agendas, and for each of us particular patients will push our buttons. Thus we learn to be slightly skeptical about ourselves, whether we feel demoralized or exhilarated after a session.

It gradually dawned on a male therapist that he responded very warmly whenever a woman patient told him she had undergone a certain type of parental neglect. After the first session, he usually envisioned a marvelous cure and outstanding achievements by the patient, whether or not this was very realistic. Eventually he learned to temper his enthusiasm and realized that his rescue fantasies related to significant events in his own past.

Countertransference in the second and broader sense includes all feelings that a therapist has regarding the patient. Many of these experiences are evoked in the therapist by the patient, and thus are an important source of data. In this sense, countertransference can be extremely helpful to a therapist, if she can use her feelings and fantasies to further her understanding of the patient.

With each patient, the therapist will feel different and experience different sorts of daydreams (fantasies) while listening. These fantasies may be fleeting or relatively persistent. It is important for the therapist to pay attention to these experiences.

With patient A on a given day, the therapist's mind wandered to thoughts of her upcoming vacation. With patient B she looked forward to what she was going to eat for lunch. Thoughts of violence (castrating a child rapist) occurred with C, while sexual thoughts occurred when her mind wandered in D's hour. With E, the therapist suddenly remembered she needed to go to the cleaners on the way home.

Each of these fantasies related to the individual patient with whom the therapist was working.

When the therapist thought about her vacation during her session with patient A, she was partly absenting herself from a rather joyless, obsessive engineer (I'd rather be snorkeling in Maui than listening to this), and partly wishing she could find some way to help her patient enjoy life more.

When the therapist thought about her upcoming lunch while with patient B, she was responding to the deep, primitive, oral needs of her regressed patient.

During patient C's session, the therapist fantasized revenge on a child rapist. Patient C had, in fact, been molested as a child, and was just becoming aware of her repressed rage.

The sexual thoughts that occurred to the therapist while she was with patient D reflected feelings of attraction the therapist felt toward her patient, and feelings that the patient was beginning to experience toward her. In fact, he expressed these in the following session.

When the therapist remembered she needed to stop at the cleaners, she was responding to patient E's venomous hostility toward everyone in her life. The patient's lack of empathy for others' experiences made the therapist feel dirty, and she looked forward to changing into a freshly cleaned outfit.

In each of the above examples, only some of the possible meanings of the countertransference fantasies of the therapist are described. Many more meanings always exist, some having more to do with the patient, some having more to do with the therapist. The important point is that the patient influences the emotional experience of the therapist in both subtle and profound ways.

It is important for the therapist to be as open as possible to her inner experience, and to consider that many meanings may be condensed into one fantasy. For example, the therapist's vacation fantasy during her session with patient A, the obsessive engineer, could have also related to the patient's memory of the one happy vacation he had ever had with his family. Or she could have been responding to his repressed fantasy of being with her on a romantic vacation.

Countertransference feelings are sometimes divided into two types (Racker 1968): (1) concordant and (2) complementary. In *concordant* countertransference, the therapist experiences what the patient feels or felt. In *complementary* countertransference, the therapist experiences what others in the patient's environment felt.

For example, with her patient C, who had been sexually abused, the therapist felt a concordant countertransference, what the patient felt—a fantasy of revenge against a child molester. At a later point in the therapy, when the patient attacked the therapist for being uncaring and even abusive, the therapist felt like the patient's caregivers might have felt (a complementary countertransference). The therapist became aware of a wish to throw the patient out. As an action, this would have constituted a present-day abuse of the patient. The therapist did not act on this impulse. Instead she processed the fantasy internally, which helped her understand the power of the patient's early experience. This experience had resulted in the patient's unconscious attempt to re-create her history of trauma with others and with the therapist.

Understanding countertransference is one important reason why even very experienced therapists consult with supervisors.

The question sometimes arises of how much to interpret based solely on countertransference. The following example is from a recent textbook of psychoanalytic technique (Etchegoyen 1991):

The analyst sneezes and then interprets that the patient feels cold and abandoned. The patient accepts this interpretation, feels that it is so, and the analyst's urge to sneeze is gone. [pp. 500–501]

Seemingly in contrast to this, Segal (1972) opined, "Countertransference is a good servant, but a poor master." By this, I believe she meant that even though countertransference may produce invaluable data, the therapist should not use it as the primary source of evidence upon which to interpret (a master). Instead, countertransference should be used to confirm, support, or hint at new ideas (a servant).

At first, countertransference may not be understood by a therapist, for example, feeling intermittently sleepy with a particular patient. In this situation the therapist may only sense that something unexpressed may be occurring in the relationship, and that she needs to remain open to its meanings. The explanation for a therapist's sleepiness might include a patient's unconsious (and therefore unexpressed) hostility, or specific factors in the therapist, such as fear (and therefore avoidance) of a patient's hostility. Regardless of its cause, sleepiness in the therapist should not result in blaming the patient.

A form of negative countertransference occurs when therapists get discouraged with the progress of therapy. Sometimes this is worse if the therapist feels constantly under attack. Borderline patients especially tend to evoke these feelings. Kernberg's (1984) clearly stated opinion is reassuring in this regard:

[The psychotherapy of borderline patients] requires intensive long-term treatment, usually not fewer than two to three sessions a week over a period of five to seven years. [p. 113]

In insight psychotherapy, contrary to opinions sometimes expressed by patients or therapists, there is no such thing as a wasted hour. Sometimes a sculptor will hit a block of marble with a hammer and chisel one hundred times in the same spot before a piece of the marble falls away. Does this mean that the first ninety-nine blows had no effect? In all circumstances, the steady perseverance of the therapist implicitly conveys a message that the effort to understand the patient is worthwhile, and that the patient is worthwhile.

Semrad gave as his opinion, "You've got to love your patients" (Rako and Mazur 1980, p. 119). What if a therapist is presented with a patient she doesn't like? First, the therapist might ask herself why she dislikes this patient. Is there transference involved? Or a projection of something she dislikes or fears in herself? Second, perhaps the patient is intentionally, though unconsciously, making himself unlikable. Finally, what if the patient were unable to find any therapist who wanted to work with him? In general, it is unconscious, rather than conscious, negative feelings in the therapist that cause the worst problems. However, if the feeling of dislike appears immovable, the therapist probably should not treat that patient.

An additional source of negative countertransference stems from the importance of the therapeutic relationship. It is easy to underestimate the importance that a therapist has in a patient's life. Conversely, recognizing that one is the most important person (at least some of the time) in the lives of ten, twenty, or thirty people can be wearing. Because it is an everyday phenomenon for the therapist, complacency sometimes creeps in, only to be abruptly driven out by a dramatic crisis in a patient's life that reaffirms the therapist's importance.

There are two ameliorating factors that can relieve some of this pressure. First, the therapist can recognize that much of the affect focused on her has its origin in transference.

Second, she can remember that her work is valuable, special, and rarely available to more than a fortunate few.

ERRORS

Errors on the part of the therapist are inevitable. "The man who doesn't make mistakes is the man who doesn't see patients," runs an old medical aphorism. ("Doctors bury their mistakes," is another.) A conscientious therapist is likely to recognize that in nearly every session she has made an error, or at least she could have done something better. These frequent errors are not dangerous. In fact, the regular discovery of errors is a characteristic of competent therapy. It is the *unrecognized, systematic errors* that occur week after week, month after month, year after year, that are damaging. These are most often detected with the aid of a supervisor.

When there has been an error that is obvious to the patient, such as the therapist forgetting an hour, ending the session early, or overcharging, the therapist should clearly admit the error, and, if appropriate, apologize. It is important to explore the patient's reactions to the error.

T: How did you react to my being twenty minutes late?

P: I think you don't want to meet with me because I'm giving you a hard time.

T: What other possibilities occur to you?

P: You might have had an emergency. Or you might have been watching your favorite soap opera.

T: I'm glad you can consider several possibilities. If I were late because I didn't want to see you, that reminds me of your father, who you said didn't want to hear any of your problems.

P: Yes, he never made time just to listen to me.

If, after exploring his own reactions, the patient again asks the therapist the meaning of her error, the therapist can assure the patient (if it is true):

T: My being late didn't have anything to do with you.

If the patient persists further in asking, the therapist faces a difficult situation. She can ask the patient what are the reasons behind his persistence. Or she can tell the patient the reasons for her error as best she understands them, and then explore the patient's reaction to that.

Greenson (1967) takes what seems like an extreme position, and recommends saying,

T: The reason for my error belongs in my therapy, not in yours. [p. 222]

STALEMATES

The term *stalemate*, borrowed from chess, implies that the patient and therapist are stuck: no change is occurring. Or the patient may be getting worse.

There are many causes for stalemates, and given the legitimate length of some therapies it is not always easy to determine when a stalemate has occurred.

One reason for a stalemate may be that the patient was not suitable for insight therapy in the first place. However, this category is like a wastebasket into which all difficult situations can by swept by a self-justifying therapist (who could then consider herself courageous for even attempting such a difficult treatment). Nevertheless, as an example, it has often been noted that insight therapy usually makes schizophrenics worse.

The most common explanation of a stalemate is that some

sort of transference–countertransference bind has occurred. The patient and therapist "push each other's buttons," so to speak, on an unconscious level. This is the opposite of the good "fit" that is so important in successful psychotherapy.

Freud (1923) described a *negative therapeutic reaction*, in which every action of the therapist that would ordinarily lead to the patient's improvement leads instead to the patient getting worse. Freud attributed this phenomenon to an unconscious sense of guilt in the patient, whose need to suffer punishment outweighed all other feelings.

In his discussion of stalemates, Kernberg (1984) described two other possibilities for negative therapeutic reactions:

> The need to destroy what is received from the therapist because of unconscious envy of him [and] the need to destroy the therapist as a good object because of the patient's unconscious identification with a primitive, sadistic object who requires submission and suffering as a minimal condition for maintaining any significant object relation. [p. 241]

These dynamics are useful to consider as causes of stalemates. However, when a therapist suspects a stalemate, supervision is a must.

WHAT IS A DYNAMIC FORMULATION?

Sometimes a supervisor will ask a therapist for her *dynamic formulation*. This phrase can be intimidating. It actually means nothing more than a statement of the therapist's understanding or hypotheses about a patient. Dynamic, in this case, refers to the therapist's ideas about the interplay of unconscious forces within the patient. If the therapist has

ideas about the patient's unconscious conflicts, these should
be included in her formulation.

Here are two examples of dynamic formulations, which
may seem redundant at this point because we have been
speaking dynamically throughout these discussions:

The patient, a 40-year-old, married assistant manufac-
turing plant manager came from a family with a domineering father who constantly belittled the patient. His
mother was relatively passive. The patient adapted by
becoming passive to authority, and somewhat afraid of
relationships with men. He struggled with repressed anger
and longing for male relationships. He was able to make
fairly good relationships with women, but there too he
struggled with passivity. In the course of therapy with a
male therapist, first his rage, and then his (partly homosexual) longings became activated in the transference.

The patient, a 38-year-old, separated legal secretary, had
been married three times, each time to a man who turned
out to be an abusive alcoholic. Her father had also been
alcoholic, and, though largely emotionally absent, had
occasionally been very warm with the patient, his favorite
daughter. The patient's mother had resented the patient,
and the relationship between the two had always been
stormy.

The patient had intense longings for affection, but
unconsciously was attracted to men who abused her.
Unconsciously these men reminded her of her father.
Furthermore, she unconsciously felt she deserved to be
abused, since she had always felt she had somehow deserved her mother's rejection. The anger she felt inside
seemed to confirm that she was "bad."

In her therapy she at first idealized her male therapist,
and felt sexually attracted to him. When he "rejected"
her, there followed a long period of expression of her

repressed rage, alternating with periods of depressive guilt feelings.

Dynamic formulations, such as these, are *always tentative*. The more possibilities the therapist can think of, the less she will have to adhere rigidly to her first ideas or favorite theories.

CHAPTER 12

Manifestations of the Unconscious: Dreams, Slips, Humor, and Psychosomatic Illness

- Dreams
- Freud's views
- Alternative approaches
- Slips of the tongue
- Humor
- Psychosomatic illness

Dreams, slips of the tongue, humor, and psychosomatic illness are all manifestations of the unconscious. Each is dealt with differently in insight therapy.

DREAMS

Sigmund Freud considered dreams to be the "royal road to the unconscious." In his seminal work, *The Interpretation of Dreams* (1900), he described his theory of dreams and a method of using them clinically. Much of his terminology and method is still used today.

Freud believed the purpose of dreams was to preserve sleep. On clinical grounds he concluded that most dreams are not remembered. Modern physiologic research on rapid eye movement (REM) sleep has confirmed that almost everyone dreams for several periods each night. It is a common occurrence that people who become interested in their dreams begin to remember dreams more frequently.

Freud called what a patient reports the *manifest content* of a dream. He called the unconscious meaning of a dream the *latent content*. Freud believed that the latent content of most dreams embodies the *fulfillment of a disguised, infantile wish*.

Wishes are disguised in dreams because of conflict within the mind. The dream censor (later identified as the superego and part of the ego) tries to enforce a strict moral code. Wishes (impulses) that are unacceptable to the dream censor reach consciousness in disguised forms. The way in which wishes are disguised to evade censorship follows certain rules of the unconscious mind.

Unconscious thought differs from logical, conscious thought. It is like another language, reflecting a primitive mode of experience. First, there is no negation—the word *no* does not exist. Anything that is mentioned in a dream is part of the dream even if the dreamer consciously rejects the idea. For example, "There was no sexual innuendo in the woman's manner." Second, opposites can coexist. For example, in a dream, a person can be both male and female. Third, there is no sense of time—a person can be young and old at the same time.

Freud identified four other characteristics of unconscious thought that govern the formation of dreams. These are condensation, displacement, symbolism, and considerations of representability.

Condensation is when two ideas or images are collapsed into one. For example, a middle-aged man's dream of a powerful railroad locomotive represented his wish for strength and stability, as well as his memory of a happy childhood train trip.

Displacement is the substitution of one similar thing for another. For example, a dream about a bus with passengers inside can represent a pregnant woman.

Symbolism refers to the occurrence of symbols in dreams, which Freud felt were universal, and could not be understood by the associative method (see below). Examples were a hat representing a penis or climbing stairs representing increasing sexual arousal.

Considerations of representability refers to the concept that dreamwork is limited by certain realistic contraints of how an idea can be represented in the dream. For example, a patient regaining hope could be represented by an angel with a halo and a wand touching a child.

Secondary revision signifies the process of making the dream more orderly and logical that goes on during the period between the experiencing of the dream and recalling it later or telling it to another person.

An immediate objection to Freud's theory of dreams as wish fulfillments concerns anxiety dreams (nightmares) and dreams of recurrent trauma. How can these represent wishes?

Freud explained anxiety dreams in an ingenious way. Since the mind contains conflicts within itself, what satisfies one part of the mind may distress another. The experience of anxiety in the dream may represent a reaction to a wish having been mentally fulfilled!

A child might have an anxiety dream about falling through space. This could symbolize being abandoned, as the result of the imaginary fulfillment of an angry wish. During the day the child felt frustrated and wished for the parent's death. This wish was expressed in the dream by the child feeling abandoned (the result of the parent's death), which also expressed the requirement of the child's superego for punishment.

It is well known that victims of trauma, for example an automobile accident, have recurrent nightmares of the event. Freud felt that these dreams were attempts at mastery. The victim was attempting to reexperience the event with a happy ending, but was overwhelmed by the reality of the trauma. This principle of repeating traumas in order to master them is seen in other clinical situations as well.

Freud's method of working on dreams was to ask the patient to associate to each element of the dream. In the following example, the patient was a 54-year-old married engineer being treated by a psychologist in his forties:

P: I dreamed I was in a courtroom being accused of theft. The prosecutor had white hair. He read a list of five points that he said proved my guilt. I'm not sure I had any pants on. I woke up very anxious.

T: What comes to mind about a courtroom?

P: Being on trial. Guilt. I was called for jury duty last year. There was a case of rape, but I wasn't selected to sit.

T: Theft?

P: I don't know. I haven't stolen anything.

T: You said the prosecutor had white hair.

P: Yes. (Pause) My father has white hair. You don't have that much hair. I hope that doesn't insult you.

T: Unfortunately that's true about my hair. What about the list of five points?

P: I don't know. I don't remember what any of them were.

T: Five points . . .

P: That was a part of the town I grew up in! Five points! The neighborhood was named because five streets converged at one intersection.

T: What comes to your mind about that neighborhood?

P: That's where Cindy lived. You know, my first girl-friend. I've talked about her before.

T: Yes. She became pregnant and you felt very guilty. What about not having any pants on?

P: I don't know. As a child I used to have dreams of being naked in public.

This patient had recently been overcoming impotence with his wife. The dream seemed to refer to his feelings of guilt associated with virile sexual performance. The theft referred to his having intercourse with Cindy when she was a virgin. The patient felt guilty for getting her pregnant.

The prosecutor resembled the patient's father, with whom he had an oedipal rivalry. The prosecutor also represented the therapist, who did not have white hair but came up in the patient's associations as losing his hair. The patient feared that the therapist judged him for getting Cindy pregnant. The patient also unconsciously saw the therapist as a critical father-rival for his wife. The patient saying that he hoped he hadn't insulted the therapist was an attempt to negate his own hostile feelings toward the therapist.

The patient's reference to his childhood dreams confirmed the multiple meanings of the dream, as it referred to his rivalry with his father as a child, his difficulties with his emerging sexuality as a late adolescent, and his current struggle for potency in the face of guilt and feared criticism from his therapist. His experience of anxiety in the dream included a reference to his current sexual anxiety with his wife.

Over the course of the session, the patient and therapist came to these understandings. However, the patient denied that he harbored any hostile feelings toward the therapist. On the contrary, he said, he felt grateful to the therapist for helping him overcome his impotence. At that point, the therapist chose not to explain that two opposite feelings (in this case gratitude and hostility) could coexist.

The redundancy of themes, easily visible in this example, is characteristic of dreams. The patient's wish was to be sexually potent, virile in all senses, and free of guilt. In this example, chosen for its relative clarity, considerable understanding was reached through the therapist's patiently asking the patient's associations to each element in the dream.

It is a frequent error to rely too heavily on the manifest content of a dream, rather than using associations to aid in uncovering the latent content. In a sense, everything a patient says in an hour that includes a dream can be considered as associations to the dream.

It is also important to remember that symbols are individual creations (Freud's opinion notwithstanding). A snake may be a phallic symbol (a traditional view), or it may represent a biting vagina. Rats (and other vermin) are frequently symbolic of siblings, but a rat can also be a phallic symbol (its hairless tail or its trait of gnawing into things).

Affects in dreams are often less disguised than thoughts or images. Thus, tears in a dream or angry feelings are more likely to correspond with the actual feelings of the dreamer. However, opposite affects occasionally occur in dreams, laughter for tears, for example.

Alternative Approaches to Dreams

Carl Jung

Jung had another view of dreams (Fordham 1953).[1] Among other meanings, Jung felt that dreams contain a message from an unconscious part of the person to the conscious part. A Jungian therapist might view the engineer's dream as a message from the "criminal" part of himself. Perhaps it had to do with his conflicted relationship with his wife. He might have been telling himself that he needed to stand up to her and with her, rather than commit the crime of depriving her sexually.

Another Jungian approach might be to consider the white-

---

[1]Jung's theories of psychotherapy also included making the unconscious conscious, although his view of the contents of the unconscious differed somewhat from Freud's.

haired prosecutor as an archetype (a sort of mythological symbol) of God. The patient's nakedness represented innocence, which he felt he had lost.

On his audiotape, Richard Johnson (1990) speaks from a Jungian spiritual perspective, "In dreams, all meals are *the meal*, and all infants are *the child*" (referring to Christian symbolism).

Gestalt Therapy

Gestalt therapists have added another technique for working with dreams (Polster and Polster 1974). This method is to ask the patient to speak from the perspective of each element of the dream. In the case of the engineer's dream the patient would be asked to speak as the prosecutor, the courtroom, and even the pair of pants. As the prosecutor the patient could accuse himself of crimes coinciding with his guilty struggles. As the courtroom, the patient might see himself as capable of being an objective evaluator. As the pants, the patient might see himself as a masculine covering or segue into discussing himself as the one who "wears the pants."

These alternative approaches have been mentioned here to show how versatile and helpful dreams can be in therapy, as well as to show how they can be approached from different viewpoints.

In practice, not all dream analyses yield helpful results. Often, only a theme rather than a specific wish can be deduced. However, working with dreams gives the patient and therapist the opportunity to rework important material, and sometimes to reach unique insights.

First Dreams

The patient's first dream in therapy is often important, frequently reflecting the patient's core conflicts. For this reason it is sometimes helpful to return to such a dream again and again.

For example, a depressed, young nurse reported her first dream:

> P: I was on an ocean liner that was nearing the dock. It was not slowing down enough and I was afraid it would crash. I woke up in a panic.

Over time, the therapist and the patient understood more meanings of this dream. As a child the patient had longed to get away from her family, which was represented by the ocean liner (about to crash = disaster). In therapy she feared getting too close to her therapist (the dock = "Doc"). She feared that either he or she would be harmed by her anger or else her "moving in on him." The theme of closeness as dangerous recurred throughout the therapy.

First dreams also frequently refer to therapy. Manifest content such as exploring a house or a wilderness may symbolize the patient exploring himself. Going under water can mean going into the unconscious. Embarking on a journey may mean the journey of therapy.

The Therapist in Dreams

Dreams can relate to the past, the present, and the transference. When a patient presents a long, complex dream and the therapist is unsure what to focus on, the transference is probably a good bet.

In dreams, the therapist is often represented by a shadowy or nondescript figure, who sometimes accompanies the patient. On a deeper level, it is possible that every person in a dream represents the therapist. Each person in a dream also represents a part of the patient.

SLIPS OF THE TONGUE

Slips of the tongue and other inadvertent acts, such as forgetting a social engagement, car keys, or to pay one's therapist, have psychological meaning (Freud 1905a).

> A young woman going out to dinner with an attractive man said, "I am simply ravished." This was a condensation of famished and ravishing. The fact that the young woman made that slip did not necessarily mean that in reality she would have a casual, sexual relationship with the man. It only meant that the impulse to do so existed within her. That impulse could easily have been of lesser strength than many others.

This example is important because although slips have meaning, they do not, as is commonly believed, reveal what the speaker really meant. They only reveal what *part* of the person meant at the time, and the strength of that part can vary.

Although patients may make revealing slips during their sessions, experience has shown that as a rule there is little clinical benefit to the therapist pointing them out. Doing so usually only provokes defensiveness. If the therapist does wish to try to make use of a patient's slip, she should try to do so gently, for example:

> T: You just said your mother when I believe you meant your wife. What meaning might that have?

Actions such as forgetting to pay should be treated in the same manner. If a patient has not paid at an agreed upon time, then the therapist could ask the patient if he is aware of his bill. If the patient has forgotten to pay, he might simply correct the oversight without comment from the therapist.

Or the therapist could ask the patient if he feels he is expressing some dissatisfaction with the therapy. (Of course, other meanings are possible, such as the patient trying to provoke the therapist to kick him out because he does not feel he deserves help, or because he is afraid, or because money has a special meaning to him, and so on.)

HUMOR

Humor is an important part of life. Ordinarily it is a serious deficit if an individual lacks a sense of humor. Many therapists have tried to help patients to accept themselves as flawed, to learn to "lighten up," or to appreciate the humor of their situations. These well-meaning therapists have tried to accomplish these goals by making humorous comments about the patients and sometimes about themselves. Almost invariably these efforts are counterproductive. Moreover, because of powerful social pressures, patients rarely tell their therapists their true reactions to humorous comments.

The use of humor in psychotherapy is fraught with difficulties. There is always a butt of a joke. If it is the patient, the laugh is at his expense. If it is the therapist, the humorous gesture may either imply insecurity or smack of false modesty. Kubie's (1971) outstanding article, "The Destructive Potential of Humor in Psychotherapy," is must reading on this subject.

Nearly all humor has either covert aggression or sexuality at its core (Freud 1905b). A major function of humor is to permit the expression of these "forbidden" sexual and aggressive impulses in a socially acceptable way. Many jokes tend to reinforce repression by supporting the idea that we can laugh at this because it is the only way we can acknowledge its truth. When a therapist makes a joke involving aggression or sexuality, she may be encouraging the patient not to deal with these impulses directly. This can obstruct the goal of insight therapy—direct awareness of one's deeper nature.

The patient is a captive audience for the humorous therapist. Even if a therapist's joke is not directly hurtful to the patient, the therapist is, in effect, showing off. If the patient is uncomfortable with the therapist's humor, he may not feel brave enough to tell her.

Of special importance with regard to humor is the history of the patient. Many patients have suffered painful ridicule as children or adolescents. These episodes may be unknown to a therapist, even after many months of therapy. A humorous therapist can unwittingly reproduce these painful experiences.

Although some humorous comments by therapists may be helpful in occasional circumstances, the risks are usually underestimated.

PSYCHOSOMATIC ILLNESS

Psychosomatic disorders are physical conditions caused or aggravated by psychologic factors (Kaplan and Sadock 1990). Illnesses generally considered to be psychosomatic include peptic ulcer, ulcerative colitis, bronchial asthma, hypertension, rheumatoid arthritis, and migraine headaches.

A large number of other diseases are affected by psychological factors. In fact, the onset of physical illness often occurs in connection with emotional events in a person's life.

Not included as psychosomatic disorders are conditions that are purely psychological, and do not cause demonstrable organic pathology. These include memory lapses, hysterical paralyses, lumps in the throat, and psychogenic pain.

Although few patients seek psychotherapy primarily for psychosomatic illnesses, many patients who seek psychotherapy for other reasons suffer from these disorders.

The general prevailing opinion is that therapy for patients with psychosomatic illnesses should be supportive rather than insight oriented. However, patients with similar physical problems may have different personality structures. There are numerous case reports of successful treatment of psychosomatic illnesses by psychodynamic therapy (Hogan 1995, for example).

There is also controversy over whether there are specific dynamics for each psychosomatic disorder versus the effects of stress in general, with the specific pathology being determined by each individual's genetically determined, susceptible organ system.

The theories advanced for the specific psychodynamics for each illness can be helpful to a therapist in thinking about her patients.

Peptic ulcer has been described as a disease in which the "hungry stomach eats itself" (Solomon and Patch 1971, p. 241). Ulcer patients frequently have deeply hidden, oral dependency needs. (The recent identification of a bacterium, *Helicobacter pylori*, as one of the causes of peptic ulcer disease [Tierney et al. 1994] complicates this traditional view.)

In *ulcerative colitis* (as well as the irritable bowel syndrome), the overactive bowel is thought to express repressed hostility through explosive diarrhea (shitting on someone). Lindemann (1944) also found a strong association between the loss of an important person and the onset of ulcerative colitis.

In *bronchial asthma*, the wheeze has been likened to a stifled cry for mother. Asthmatic patients are said to struggle with deeply rooted dependency needs and intense separation anxiety. Because severe asthma attacks can be fatal, aggressive medical treatment of asthma should be recommended.

Hypertension (high blood pressure) has many organic causes. However, so-called *essential hypertension* is thought to be associated with overly controlled, suppressed rage.

In *rheumatoid arthritis*, it has been said that the patient is "able to get his hostility out only as far as his fists" (Solomon and Patch 1971, p. 244). Chronic anger, stress, and loss have all been implicated in the psychological causes of this debilitating disease.

"A murder a day keeps the migraine away," runs an old German saying (Solomon and Patch 1971, p. 245). *Migraines* have been linked to stress and deeply repressed hostility.

Eating disorders are not strictly considered psychosomatic, but the somatic consequences of both anorexia nervosa and bulimia can be severe. Patients with these disorders may be severely disturbed. Issues of control and independence and complex family dynamics are the rule.

If a psychotherapy patient has one of these psychosomatic illnesses, it can be helpful for the therapist to consider the role of the illness in the person's life and inner world, including secondary gain (for example, attention, sympathy, disability payments). However, it is generally best not to interpret the illness or symptoms directly. When this is attempted, the patient usually feels attacked and becomes defensive.

For example, if a patient has bronchial asthma, understanding that the patient may have strong dependency needs can be helpful in guiding the therapist's attention, but the "cause" of an asthma attack should not be labeled by the therapist. Similarly, in working with a patient with migraine, a therapist should interpret hostility only when it is clearly present in the patient's material. The therapist should *not* say, "You got a headache because of your repressed anger."

Instead of interpreting psychosomatic symptoms, it is best

to leave them as "markers" of how the patient is progressing. If the patient is becoming more aware of his repressed feelings, it is likely that his symptoms will improve. Furthermore, sometimes the patient will discover a meaning of his illness for himself. If he does, this will be more effective than the therapist's interpretations.

The relationship of the mind and body is complex, and ultimately there is only one whole being. Psychotherapy patients may develop organic illnesses. A patient with a brain tumor may dream that he has a brain tumor. On the other hand, there are numerous anecdotal reports of patients' eyeglass prescriptions changing as they "see" more clearly as a result of their therapy.

CHAPTER 13

Dealing with Grief

- The grief syndrome
- Treatment

God, please grant me:
the serenity to accept the things I cannot change,
the courage to change the things I can,
and the wisdom to know the difference.

The Serenity Prayer (adapted from Niebuhr 1934)

Insight therapy is aimed at helping people to realize what they can change, and to accept what they cannot. A good interpretation has the effect of helping a patient sort out these alternatives. Thus, one effect of insight is an *enhanced ability to change*.

The assistant plant manager who had felt bullied by his boss was helped by his therapist's interpretations to see that he had options for the future other than continued submission.

In her therapy, the woman who had married three alcoholic husbands realized that she had been unconsciously choosing men who would abuse her. This and other insights helped her form new and better relationships.

A second effect of insight is the *recognition of loss*. Accepting past and present reality with its painful losses implies *grief*.

The assistant plant manager needed to mourn the years of oppression by his father, his thwarted yearnings for acceptance and affirmation, and the stultifying effect of these experiences on the development of his character. Furthermore, although he had come to recognize he had many options, some opportunities had already passed him by.

The woman who married alcoholic men had to mourn both her childhood abuse, and the painful chaos of her recent years.

Dealing with grief occupies an important role in all depth psychotherapies. Every patient who sees a therapist has already experienced significant losses. As the patient's view of reality becomes clearer, inevitably there is a recognition of more losses. With many patients, a major task for the therapist is to help the patient mourn.

In a classic article, Lindemann (1944) described the process of grief. Although he focused on bereavement, his insights are valuable in relation to all grieving, including that which occurs in therapy. He made the following points:

1. Acute grief is a definite syndrome with psychological and somatic symptomatology.
2. This syndrome may appear immediately after a crisis; it may be delayed; it may be exaggerated or, apparently absent.
3. In place of the typical syndrome there may appear distorted pictures . . .

4. By appropriate techniques these distorted pictures can be successfully transformed into a normal grief reaction with resolution. [p. 141]

Lindemann found the symptomatology of acute grief to be remarkably uniform, consisting of

sensations of somatic distress occurring in waves lasting from twenty minutes to an hour at a time, a feeling of tightness in the throat, choking with shortness of breath, need for sighing, and an empty feeling in the abdomen, lack of muscular power, and an intense subjective distress described as tension or mental pain. The patient soon learns that these waves of discomfort can be precipitated by visits, by mentioning the deceased, and by receiving sympathy. There is a tendency to avoid the syndrome at any cost, to refuse visits, lest they should precipitate the reaction, and to keep deliberately from thought all references to the deceased. [p. 141]

Lindemann felt that six points comprised the *grief syndrome*:

1. Somatic distress (described above)
2. Preoccupation with the image of the deceased
3. Guilt, centered around having harmed or not having done right by the deceased
4. Hostile reactions, sometimes toward people in general, sometimes toward specific persons (such as doctors)
5. Loss of patterns of conduct, resulting in aimless activity, and a readiness to depend on anyone who will direct the actions of the bereaved person
6. The appearance of traits of the deceased in the behavior of the bereaved. [p. 142]

Lindemann found that the duration of a grief reaction depended on the success with which a person did the *grief work*. He described this work as

emancipation from bondage to the deceased, readjustment to the environment in which the deceased was missing, and the formation of new relationships . . . One of the big obstacles to this work seems to be the fact that *many patients try to avoid the intense distress connected with the grief experience and to avoid the expression of emotion necessary for it.* [p. 143, emphasis added]

Next, Lindemann described various types of *morbid grief reactions*, including delayed and distorted reactions. *Delayed reactions* occurred anywhere from days to years later. It is a common experience for patients in therapy to discover that they have stored up grief inside from important losses long ago. One example is the reawakening of feelings of loss over having given up a child for adoption many years previously. Anniversary reactions, in which a person experiences grief on the date of a previous loss, can be especially striking.

Distorted grief reactions occurred in various forms. These included changes in personality, hypomania, severe depression, and, at times, the onset of a psychosomatic disease such as rheumatoid arthritis, asthma, and especially, ulcerative colitis. Lindemann also reported that the course of the ulcerative colitis was strikingly improved when the grief reaction was resolved with professional help.

When discussing *treatment*, Lindemann stated very clearly, "The essential task facing the psychiatrist is that of *sharing the patient's grief work*" (p. 147, emphasis added). *Sharing* implies participating in the patient's emotional experience. The therapist must help the patient bear the pain of reviewing his relationship to the deceased. The patient needs to verbalize all of his feelings, including those of guilt. He needs to find new patterns of rewarding social interaction.

The expression of affect, to a receptive listener, is essential. This part of the grief work is sometimes the most difficult for both patient and therapist.

A man accidentally caused the death of his small daughter. With his therapist he was able to describe the event over and over, sometimes with shaking sobs. Frequently the patient voiced the fear that he was wearing out his therapist. Perhaps neither party looked forward to the sessions. After a considerable period of time the patient resumed being able to sleep, and was able to participate fully in life again.

Therapists who have not worked through important losses in their own lives will be unable to "stay with" patients who must face these issues.

Common errors of beginning therapists in dealing with grief are

1. changing the subject,
2. pointing out that the glass is half full instead of half empty, or otherwise trying to cheer the patient up,
3. sharing personal experiences of loss,
4. interpreting anger too early or at the wrong time.

Grief occurs not only after a death, but after losses of any kind. Examples include the ending of a relationship, or the loss of a limb, a job, a prized ability, an ideal, or an opportunity. In each case the patient must review his relationship with the lost object, readjust to reality without it, and form new relationships. Again, the experiencing and expression of affect is essential.

An athletic man lost a leg in a car accident. As a result, he could no longer run or ski. During the course of his psychotherapy, he reminisced about his enjoyment of sports and the medals he had won. He told his therapist how hard it was for him not to be able to move about quickly and to stick with his physical therapy. Finally, he began to share the details about his new hobby, fly fishing. All of this was told with the expression of genuine feelings, and he made a good recovery.

A 44-year-old woman was left by her husband, who took up with a much younger woman. The patient's anger gradually turned to sadness, as she mourned the loss of what she had felt to be a good marriage. In time, she was able to see the weaknesses of the marriage as well. As she expressed her sorrow with her therapist, she became more open to new relationships.

If a patient seems unable to grieve, it is sometimes helpful to ask,

> T: How do you deal with losses?

If the patient recognizes he has difficulties in this area, the therapist can add,

> T: Perhaps you never had anyone to help you with them.

Or,

> T: Perhaps you never had anyone to share them with you.

Referring to grief, Semrad (Rako and Mazer 1980) commented:

Laymen often think that the best way to deal with any difficult situation is *not* to deal with it—to forget it. But you and I have the experience that the only way you can forget is to remember. [p. 106]

The purpose of this chapter has been to emphasize the important role of the insight therapist in helping patients grieve by sharing their grief work.

Treating
Depression

Kubœe 1971. The ~~destructive~~
potential of humor in
psychotherapy.

- Developmental issues
- A view of depression
- The psychotherapy of depression

Depression can be a syndrome, an illness, an affect, a mood, a feeling, a symptom, or a character style. It has never been satisfactorily defined (Basch 1975). Some feelings of depression, like anxiety, are a part of life. However, *depression may be the most common complaint among psychotherapy patients*. Furthermore, during the course of depth psychotherapy, many patients experience increased feelings or symptoms of depression.

Some depressions appear to have purely physical causes, for example those associated with specific diseases (e.g., hepatitis, hypothyroidism) or with the side effects of certain drugs (e.g., corticosteroids, reserpine). Other depressions have mixed biological and psychosocial causes, for example, the depressions that occur in bipolar (manic-depressive) illness. Many depressions appear to be primarily the result of psychological events. The principles outlined in this chapter apply to treating most forms of depression. (See Chapter 10 for a discussion of referral for medications.)

Depression is emphasized here because of its relation to grief, its ubiquity, and the fact that inexperienced therapists often find it difficult to work with depressed patients.

Depression evokes powerful feelings in therapists, who, understandably, want to relieve their patients' pain. Yet trying directly to lift the patient's mood may not be helpful. By the time most patients have arrived at a therapist's office, they have been told by relatives and friends (and by themselves):

"Things are not so bad."
"Look at the bright side."
"Snap out of it."
"You just need to try."
"You just need to trust in the Lord."

If the therapist says similar things, it may make the patient feel worse because, of course, he cannot comply. Furthermore, because of the guilt associated with depression, being nice to a patient may also make him feel worse. A senior hospital psychiatrist used to say, "The best thing that can happen to a depressed patient is to get a traffic ticket on the way home from the hospital."

There are many ways of working with depressed patients. Cognitive therapy (Beck et al. 1979) addresses the "depressed colored glasses" with which the depressed patient views the world. The cognitive therapist attempts to help the patient realistically evaluate his situation and accurately judge the effects of his efforts, which the therapist encourages. The therapist is very active. Positive transference is exploited rather than interpreted.

Insight therapists make partial use of similar techniques, for example, helping patients realize their actual capabilities even though they are depressed (by pointing out passive–active reversals, see below). These aspects of cognitive therapy resemble what psychoanalysts call working with the ego (that part of the mind that is oriented toward external reality).

Rather than trying to lift the patient's mood by encouragement, praise, or reassurance, an insight therapist attempts to understand the patient, while providing a psychologically holding environment. She may attempt to encourage the patient, to foster hope as a way of furthering their work together. However, a central part of the therapist's work consists of listening and trying to understand the patient.

Meyersburg and colleagues (1974) formulated a useful clinical approach to depression in a paper entitled, "A Reverberating Psychic Mechanism in the Depressive Processes." The following discussion is a summary of their ideas.

DEVELOPMENTAL ISSUES

The physical helplessness of the infant necessitates consistent, devoted care for its survival. A very intense bond develops between the baby and its mother (or other caregivers). The disruption of this bond is the primary threat to an infant's sense of security and survival.

A child responds to his mother's absence with intense anxiety. For relief, the child may fantasize the mother's reappearance. When this is unsuccessful and her absence continues (producing mounting distress), the child may avoid the feeling of helpless need by fantasizing that he has caused her disappearance—that his neediness has driven her away or that his angry impulses have killed her. *It may feel better for a human being to believe that he is the cause of something bad happening to him than to believe that he is truly powerless.* "This technique of turning a passive experience into an active one is a fundamental principle of early mental functioning" (Meyersburg et al. 1974, p. 373).

Thus, early in life the child may experience himself as

omnipotent. Whatever happens is the result of his needs and his actions (including the mental action of wishing). And it is true that much of a very young child's world does in fact revolve around him ("his majesty the baby"). In this vein, Winnicott (1965) writes that the mother's first task is to "illusion" her infant (that the world will provide for his needs); her second task is to "disillusion" the infant (to help him to accept that it may not).

Feelings of omnipotence can lead to uncontrolled behavior in a child (I can have anything I want, *right now*!). At this stage of development, impulsivity, omnipotence strivings, and perfectionism (I can have *everything* I want) are coextensive.

As development progresses, it becomes necessary for the parents to set limits on the child's behavior. This limit-setting process is extremely frustrating for the child. The child must be able to express his frustration within the context of his relationship with his parents.

A toddler became determined to stick a hairpin into an electric wall outlet. The parents did not allow the behavior, which resulted in a temper tantrum. At this point the parental task was to help the toddler experience his feelings without damaging himself or anyone else, without feeling rejected by his parents, or concluding that he or his feelings were "bad." In this situation, the father picked up the screaming child and held him firmly but soothingly against his chest until the child calmed down.

Thus the father helped the child learn to contain his emotions without damage. Support for the child during these experiences conveys the message: "Yes, it is painful to want what you can't have. You are not bad for having feelings of loss and anger." Through these experiences the child learns to distinguish between punitive issues (stemming from parental rejection or dislike) and limit-setting processes (constructive parental directiveness). As limits are accepted, the fantasy of omnipotence is gradually relinquished, and the child learns to accept people and relationships that are imperfect.

Insufficient support for the child's emotional experience during the time of limit setting will reinforce an ever more frantic need for omnipotence and perfection.

If a child feels responsible for experiences of deprivation (through active–passive reversals), he will feel something like guilt. "Failure of help from others is equated with failure of self-help. Self-blame results. . . . If early impulsivity and omnipotence strivings are insufficiently mastered, unexpected severe losses and disappointments of other sorts will lead to a sense of guilt" (Meyersburg et al. 1974, pp. 375–376).

Thus, a child who has experienced early deprivations and trauma may experience guilt instead of grief. A child only learns to grieve with the help of adults.

A VIEW OF DEPRESSION

Passive–active reversals are frequently observed in depressed adults. Depressed patients feel overwhelmed and preoccupied by circumstances they cannot control, while they fail to act to change the things they can. In extreme cases, depressed individuals feel responsible for international catastrophes, while at the same time they feel unable to get out of bed!

The normal reaction to loss or traumatic events is grief (see Chapter 13). Depressed individuals suffer from an inability to grieve—to accept helplessness, to feel sadness and anger—and to work through their losses. Instead of grieving, a depressed person becomes confused about reality through passive–active reversals. He cannot accurately assess what he is helpless about and what he can change. Primarily, he feels that he has failed. There is a regression to childhood experiences of impulsivity, perfectionism, guilt, and self-punitiveness. This reverberating, depressogenic psychic process is illustrated in Figure 14–1.

These behaviors—impulsivity, perfectionism, guilt, and self-punitiveness—are easily observable in depressed patients. The use of the word *should* usually indicates perfectionism and guilt. For example:

P: I should not be so upset about not getting that promotion.

P: I should not let myself be affected by things that happened years ago.

Many patients live in a chronic state of depression as evidenced by persistent impulsiveness, for example, addicts and borderline patients. For these individuals, the self-punitive remorse that sometimes follows impulsive actions is the next step in the depressogenic cycle.

THE PSYCHOTHERAPY OF DEPRESSION

Important elements in the psychotherapy of depression are (1) helping patients grieve, and (2) clarifying reality, including the patient's view of his own abilities, so that he is able to act effectively.

The therapist should direct her comments toward interrupting the depressogenic cycle. If all four elements of the cycle are present, the therapist should focus first on the patient's impulsiveness. This behavior is most likely to cause immediate problems for the patient (and may threaten the therapy). Some patients do not recognize their patterns of

Figure 14–1. The Reverberating Depressogenic Process

Normal Response Pattern
to Traumatic Experience

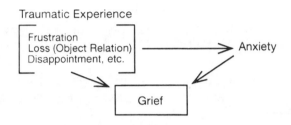

Depressogenic Mechanism

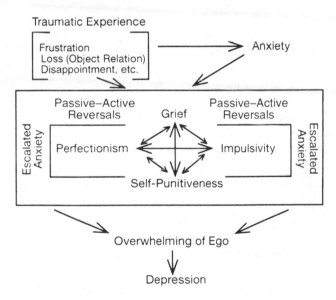

Reprinted from "A Reverberating Psychiatric Mechanism in the Depressive Processes" by H.A. Meyersburg, S.L. Ablon, and J. Kotin, in *Psychiatry* 1974, 37:372–386 and used by permission of *Psychiatry*.

acting impulsively. Even when the therapist points it out, they can scarcely imagine any other way of being.

> T: It seems to me that you are a very impulsive person. What sort of problems does this cause for you?
>
> P: I've always acted on my feelings.
>
> T: What would happen if you felt your feelings for a while before you acted?

Perfectionism, guilt, and self-punitiveness can be spotlighted whenever they occur. Almost any expression of guilt includes perfectionistic expectations.

> P: My putting up with my husband's abuse for so long was harmful to my children.
>
> T: Yet there were reasons for your staying in that relationship, both external and internal. It's perfectionistic to think that you could have just skipped over that stage in your development.

If a patient curtails his impulsiveness, and ceases to blame himself for his losses, his grief may become evident. The therapist helps the patient to recognize his grief, and then helps him work it through.

Depressed patients have an inability to be sad (a major part of grief). Such patients may have been told that when they cry they are "just feeling sorry for themselves." A major difference between *sadness* (which is a part of grief) and *depression* is that depressed patients have low self-esteem, whereas this is not an essential part of sadness, however painful. Freud (1917) expressed this thought:

> In mourning [grief] it is the world which has become poor and empty; in melancholia [depression] it is the ego itself. [p. 246]

Patients are often surprised to learn that sadness and depression are not the same. However, once this distinction is understood, they can often readily distinguish between the two. First, patients can recognize the difference in their self-esteem. Second, depression is often described as a feeling of heaviness or oppression, in contrast to sadness, which is painful in a different way, and may be accompanied by tears. Once patients recognize sadness, the therapist can share in the grief work.

Many people have not had the experience of doing grief work in their own families. This was not because the parents were mean, but because they did not want their children to suffer.

The night before her junior prom, a 16-year-old girl received a call from the boy who was to take her, saying that he was canceling their date. The girl was devastated. She seriously considered taking an overdose of sleeping pills. Then she decided that she would never date again, and vowed to become a nun.

Her distraught parents considered (1) taking her for a vacation in Hawaii to make up for her loss, (2) going to talk to the boy's parents, (3) calling her cousin to take her to the dance, (4) suing the boy for the cost of the new dress and shoes, (5) telling her that the boy was a jerk anyway, that there were lots more fish in the sea, and that she shouldn't get so upset. All of these responses pointed to an external solution, and would not have helped the girl deal with herself internally.

Instead of any of the above reactions, both parents sat on the couch next to the girl. Her mother held her hand, and her father said, "You can just sit here with us and cry as long as you need to."

The girl remembered that bittersweet night the rest of her life.

242   Getting Started

The example above illustrates a helpful family response. A 45-year-old woman who had just been told she had breast cancer would have similar needs.

A key element of grief work is accepting helplessness. This is never easy for anyone. The patient's ability to do this, promoted by the therapist's affective attunement, is a sign of progress.

Limit setting may also be a feature of psychotherapy with depressed patients. This may arise with regard to fees, hours, or the withholding of various gratifications by the therapist. Patients' responses frequently echo their experiences with limits as a child. The patient's task in therapy is roughly the same as the child's in earlier circumstances: accepting the limits without withdrawal or a fall in self-esteem, and dealing with the feelings of frustration that accompany the imposition of limits.

A depressed patient's anger at his therapist may be a valuable experience for a number of reasons, including (1) the expression of anger as an activity (as opposed to depressive withdrawal), (2) transference reexperience (of repressed anger at parents, which may require interpretation), and (3) the patient's experience of the therapist's response. The therapist does not retaliate and remains committed to the patient. Thus the patient learns that his angry feelings are acceptable and not necessarily destructive.

Depressed patients are often angry. This is an understandable reaction to disappointment and loss. Anger may also be turned inward on the self for a variety of reasons, including guilt.

Grieving is one of two tasks for a depressed person. The other task is to act in his own behalf (although this often includes generosity to others). It is important for the therapist to point out passive–active reversals. Not only does this reduce guilt and self-blame, but awareness of passive–active reversals helps the patient assess reality in terms of his potential actions.

A depressed patient usually feels helpless and hopeless—that he is a powerless victim who can do nothing to change his situation. The therapist must help the patient see that he has options.

Seeking the help of a therapist is an action, as is grieving. Thus every psychotherapy patient is already performing a powerful action in his own behalf. That this endeavor (coming to therapy) is not instantly successful is itself an occasion for grief. However, the patient's perseverance in his therapy, as well as performing his grief work, should be acknowledged by his therapist as important constructive actions.

Not only is the patient already performing some constructive actions, but almost always, the patient has more options. For a severely depressed person, one option might be literally to get out of bed, or to do one thing inside the house and one thing outside the house each day. For patients who are able to function, options might include starting to attend church, asking for a raise, or making new social contacts. Optimally, the patient and therapist will discover these choices together.

An additional way the therapist helps the patient enhance his capacity for action is by helping him to enlarge his horizons. Many depressed patients have narrowed visions of what they can accomplish. The therapist encourages the patient to explore the full extent of his fantasy life.

> T: I realize you are devastated by the loss of your girlfriend. This is certainly an occasion for grief, and we are doing important work in dealing with your feelings of loss. Besides her return, what would you like to happen to you?
>
> P: I can't think of anything.
>
> T: There must be something. A new and better relationship? A promotion? Winning the lottery? You don't have to stay within the bounds of reality to fantasize.

If the patient's internal freedom is enlarged, he is more likely to consider new options. Furthermore, even if his wishes are unrealistic, he will feel supported by the therapist who listens and accepts his dreams.

This chapter is not intended as a comprehensive guide to the treatment of depression. It is only intended to offer a few approaches a beginning therapist might use in dealing with the difficult problems presented by depressed patients.

In working with depressed patients, a therapist can keep in mind a slightly modified version of the Serenity Prayer:

God, please grant me:
the ability to grieve for the things I cannot change,
the courage to change the things I can,
and the wisdom to know the difference.

CHAPTER 15

Suicide and Homicide

- Assessment
- Working with the patient

SUICIDE

Assessment of Risk

When suicide is a possibility, either because the patient has brought it up or because the therapist suspects it, the therapist's first task is assessment of the risk.

The therapist needs to ask the patient if he is suicidal, if he intends to harm himself. Most of the time, patients will tell their therapists if they are suicidal. Naturally, the better the relationship between the two, the more open the patient will be.

If the patient says yes in any form, the therapist might then ask:

T: Do you intend to do it? How? When?

These questions are part of the assessment, and each answer the patient gives helps the therapist understand the situation better. For example, the patient might say:

P: Yes, I am thinking about killing myself, but I'm not going to.

If the therapist is not convinced, she can ask:

T: What would make you do it? How would you do it? Where?

A different patient might say:

P: I'm thinking about suicide, but I know I wouldn't do it.

T: Yes. Thinking about it isn't the same as doing it. And hearing your thoughts about it can help us.

The therapist still might proceed to explore the patient's fantasies:

T: How would you do it if you were going to?

Or,

T: How come you wouldn't do it?

The therapist can also ask,

T: How worried about you should I be?

In the above example, the therapist encouraged the patient to talk about his suicidal fantasies. Inexperienced therapists sometimes shy away from this topic, which then goes underground.

If the patient says he is thinking about suicide but is not sure if he will do it or not, might do it, and so on, or if the therapist is unsure of the situation for any reason, then the following risk factors can be helpful in the assessment:

History

The patient's history is the best guide. Past attempts increase
the risk of another attempt. The more serious the previous
attempt(s), the greater the risk. For example, three previous
overdoses of five to ten sleeping pills is less ominous than
one previous overdose of fifty pills requiring hospitalization
on an intensive care unit.

Method

Does the patient have a method in mind? How lethal is it
likely to be? Does the patient have the means at hand? Is
anyone likely to rescue the patient? The more specific the
plan, the greater the danger. For example, a patient who
says, "I'm going to kill myself but I'm not sure how," or,
"I'll take pills," but upon questioning doesn't currently have
any pills, is far less lethal than a man who says he is going to
a specific place to shoot himself with a loaded gun already in
his possession.

Other Risk Factors

The following are associated with higher risk:

1. male gender
2. older age group
3. living alone
4. separated, divorced, or widowed
5. unemployed
6. reunion after death fantasy
7. psychosis (especially hallucinations of command)
8. family history of suicide, especially immediate family
   members
9. special circumstances, such as terminal illness
10. lack of religion or life meaning.

If a patient says he will not harm himself, and the therapist still thinks the patient is suicidal, the situation is far more complex. The patient may be chaotic or even psychotic. It is unlikely that there is a good relationship between the therapist and the patient: an adversarial relationship may exist. If in this situation, the therapist is convinced that the patient is likely to harm himself, the therapist must take action. An immediate consultation (a second opinion) might be suggested (if it is feasible and the patient is willing) or else involuntary hospitalization may be required.

What To Do

It is important to remember that since the patient is currently alive, part of him wants to live. People kill themselves when they feel hopeless, and when they have lost connection with another person. Therefore, the therapist's strategies are aimed at these basic positions.

The therapist needs to feel enough in contact with the patient so that she can work with him. *A clearly understood agreement that the patient will call for help if he feels close to acting on his suicidal impulses is almost a necessity.* The therapist can also offer temporary hospitalization to the patient. This may reassure the patient that there is something more that can be done if necessary.

The attitude of the therapist that she expects the patient to improve and plans to work with him through this crisis is of inestimable value. The therapist's attitude instills hope in the patient. Because of the depth of the patient's despair, he may need more contact (connection) with the therapist than usual during a suicidal crisis. Depending on the therapist's tolerance, she may suggest to the patient that he call her at regular intervals through the crisis. This could be as often as daily or even every few hours for short periods.

It is better if the patient makes the calls, since that reinforces activity and purpose. It is easier for the therapist if she makes herself available at a specific time to receive the patient's calls. (Of course, if the patient fails to call, then she must call him.) As the crisis wanes, the frequency of calls can be tapered.

This intense contact accomplishes several things. It structures the patient's existence when he lacks his own resources to do so. It communicates the hopefulness of the therapist. And it gives the patient a new connection when he lacks any.

Some therapists make contracts with patients that the patient will not commit suicide before the next appointment. This may be another version of the therapist making herself important to the patient. However, it may feel coercive to the patient, who may comply temporally but not feel understood.

If a suicidal patient unexpectedly calls a therapist, the therapist can honestly say, "I'm glad you called." This is always true, since the alternative might be a completed suicide. At times the therapist is reduced to saying:

> T: You need to do something to occupy yourself right now. We can work on your longer-term issues when we meet for our next session. What can you do until we can talk again? Why don't you call me in three hours and let me know how you are doing?

A therapist cannot maintain this level of contact for too long, especially since crises are most likely to occur at the worst points in a therapist's life, for example when she is taking her Ph.D. exams! However, this approach may give the patient and therapist enough time to begin working through the crisis. If not, hospitalization may be required.

Not all therapists would agree with this level of involvement beyond regularly scheduled hours. It is entirely reasonable for a therapist to tell a patient that if he becomes suicidal, he can go to a hospital emergency room for evaluation at any time. Therapists who hold this position might also be more likely to hospitalize a patient during a suicidal crisis. All therapists should make sure that they have on-call coverage for nights, weekends, and vacations.

With highly suicidal patients, immediate hospitalization may be required in any case. It is a general principle of managing suicidal patients to *share the risk*. This may be done with a colleague or supervisor, the staff of a hospital to which the patient has been admitted, and with the patient's family. If the therapist believes the patient is in danger of immediate self-destruction, she must take all possible measures, including calling the paramedics or the police.

Working with a Suicidal Patient

Carl Whitaker (1969) stated, "Suicide is always a two person event." Freud (1917) wrote, "No neurotic harbors thoughts of suicide, which he has not turned back upon himself from murderous impulses against others" (p. 252). If these statements are true, the question for the patient and therapist is, Who is the other person?

Sometimes the answer to this question is obvious, for example, in the case of a suicidal jilted lover. However, there is usually someone behind the lover in the patient's past—a parent, for example. At the height of the transference neurosis, the other person may be the therapist.

As the patient recognizes his rage at the other person(s), he is likely to become less self-destructive. The connection between anger and self-destructiveness may also be manifested in the patient's sequence of associations. First, he voices his anger, then he talks of suicide (perhaps on the basis of guilt). The patient may be unaware of this sequence until the therapist points it out.

It is important to explore in depth the patient's fantasies of his suicide. What does he think will happen to him? What does he fantasize will be the reaction of others? Of the therapist? Often suicidal patients are regressed, and do not think clearly about the consequences of their proposed action. It is sometimes helpful to remind a suicidal parent of the "proven fact" that his suicide will irreparably damage his children, and increase manyfold the chances of their committing suicide.

As long as suicide is an issue, the therapist must continually focus on it. For example:

> T: Well, you are talking about law school . . . although I guess killing yourself is still a possibility . . .

Furthermore, taking seriously a patient's contemplation of suicide communicates respect for the patient. No matter how unlikely and manipulative a suicidal threat seems, it should always merit the therapist's serious attention.

If a patient has made an actual suicide attempt, it is important to work on repairing the relationship. First, the therapist must deal with her own countertransference, which probably includes angry feelings toward the patient. Next, she must try to understand the patient's experience—what were his thoughts and feelings before and after his act. Finally, the patient is likely to feel frightened and ashamed:

> P: (Thoughts) I am too much for my therapist. She is probably angry and doesn't want to work with me. I feel ashamed of my vulnerability and neediness. Even as a suicide I am a failure.

When a patient can truly renounce suicide, he has turned an important corner in his therapy. It requires strength for a person in pain to commit to facing life. The therapist may choose to acknowledge this event when it occurs. The patient may also need to mourn the loss of his "escape hatch."

Working with chronically suicidal patients can be draining. Sometimes the therapist is the keeper of that part of the patient that wants to live. If a therapist is going to work with chronically suicidal patients, she must accept the possibility that in spite of her best efforts, a patient may commit suicide. If a therapist is too fearful of her patient killing himself, she will, in effect, be an emotional hostage, and will not be able to function optimally. In this situation, the therapist will feel more and more resentful.

> [Statistically] the average professional psychologist involved in direct patient care has a better than one in five chance of losing a patient to suicide at some time during his or her professional career, with the odds climbing to better than 50–50 for psychiatrists. [Bongar 1991; p. x]

If a therapist does have a patient who commits suicide, it is important that he or she work through her grief by discussing the case with other people.

If a therapist keeps notes on a patient's therapy, the legal issues surrounding suicide can be worrisome. It is important that the therapist show her thinking in the patient's chart. For example, if the patient agrees to come to his next appointment or to call the therapist if he becomes more self-destructive, that would militate against an immediate suicide and should be noted. If in the therapist's opinion the patient is not immediately suicidal, she can write, "The patient is not suicidal now."

Most suicidal crises are relatively short lived, and patients who survive them are glad that they did not die.

HOMICIDE

Assessment of Risk

When a patient threatens to harm someone, the therapist naturally discusses it with the patient. What is the patient's wish? fantasy? plan? actual intention? Does the patient have the means available? Has he taken steps in reality? The more specific the plan, and if concrete steps have been taken (for example, buying a gun), the higher the likelihood of violence.

The most accurate predictor of violence is an individual's past history. Has the patient committed violent acts before? Other high-risk factors include a history of other antisocial acts, substance abuse, exposure to violence, hallucinations of command, and lack of social supports.

Most patients can discuss the reasons for their homicidal wishes. However, homicidal patients are often regressed, and do not think clearly about the consequences of their proposed actions. Discussions of the likely consequences of violence for the patient are frequently helpful. The patient may then be able to see less destructive ways of expressing his feelings.

The Duty to Warn

If the therapist believes a patient is likely to harm someone, in many states the therapist is legally required to warn that person. Furthermore, the therapist must do all she can, consistent with her own safety, to prevent the crime. This legal requirement generally coincides with good clinical practice.

Although it may be difficult, it is probably best for the therapist to tell the patient she is warning his potential victim. Preferably, the call should be made with the patient in the room. In the long run, the patient will usually understand the situation, and may be reassured by the therapist's clearheadedness.

Working with a Homicidal Patient

The patient sharing his homicidal impulses with the therapist represents a wish for help. The therapist's calm demeanor and steady commitment to the patient can be very helpful at this time.

The patient is most likely to be violent during periods of intense excitement, poor judgment, and impaired impulse control. Therefore, the therapist can help the patient plan to avoid situations where emotional upsets are likely.

Other helpful actions include encouraging the patient to avoid alcohol and drugs and to be with responsible friends or family as much as possible. The patient should be encouraged to share his feelings with others if he feels safe in doing so. This will help him work through the hurtful event(s) that have led to his rage.

The therapist can help the patient find alternatives to violence during periods of upset. These can include making an agreement with the patient that he should call her (as well as reliable others) if he feels like he will lose control. Keeping in close contact with the patient by telephone during the crisis may be very helpful. Other common sense options include the patient's immediately leaving escalating, stressful situations. Leaving the area is sometimes helpful.

If she feels comfortable, the therapist might take active measures, such as asking the patient to give her his gun for safekeeping (if the patient has no one else to whom he can give it).

As the crisis wanes, the patient and therapist can work on understanding the deeper meaning of the episode for the patient. How can the patient become less vulnerable? Did the precipitating event reproduce a prior trauma? What was the patient's role in setting himself up? As with anything else in depth psychotherapy, an attitude of investigation is essential.

Threats to the Therapist

A therapist cannot work without a feeling of personal safety. If a therapist receives a direct threat from a patient, or if she suspects a patient of intending violence toward her, she may decide that she cannot work with that patient any longer. "Don't be a hero," is the conventional wisdom. Consultation with a supervisor or colleague is a must. If at all possible it is important to tell the patient:

> T: Part of this may be me, and part of it may be you, but I feel afraid of you. To be fair to you, and to me, I can't continue to work with you. Here are the names of some therapists [or clinics] I can recommend.

The therapist may need to have someone else in the room when she tells the patient she feels afraid and can no longer work with him. However, because of its honesty, telling the patient directly is unlikely to make an attack more likely. Instead, it may help the patient recognize his effect on other people.

A threat to the therapist is one of the rare situations where a sudden termination is recommended (see Chapter 16).

CHAPTER 16

The Ending Phase
of Psychotherapy

- Deciding when to stop
- Goals of the ending phase
  1. Review and recapitulation
  2. Dealing with the end of the relationship; saying goodbye

DECIDING WHEN TO STOP

Common sense suggests that the ending[1] phase of therapy should occur when the stated goals of treatment have been reached. Sometimes this is the case, for example, when a patient has recovered from a depression. At other times, the initial symptoms that brought the patient into treatment have been relieved, but new treatment goals have arisen:

After six months of twice weekly therapy a 35-year-old accountant no longer felt severely depressed. He had more energy and his functioning at work had improved. How-

---

[1]The word *termination* is traditionally used for ending psychotherapy. I feel the word *ending* has fewer unpleasant connotations, but following custom, I will use the words interchangeably.

ever, he increasingly realized that he had chronic difficulties with intimate relationships. These now became the focus of his therapy.

Besides symptom relief and the achievement of treatment goals, another criterion for termination is the ability of the patient to engage in self-inquiry and self-evaluation. At this point, the patient no longer needs the therapist's help to continue the process of observing and understanding himself. *This achievement may be the most important accomplishment of the therapy.*

If a patient proposes ending the therapy, the therapist usually suggests that they discuss it. The therapist can ask the patient what has led to her decision, how she will feel on her own, if she will feel free to return, and so on. This sort of investigation is especially important because of the frequency with which other issues, such as negative transference, are expressed by the wish to stop coming.

It is not always easy, even for an experienced therapist, to know when some patients should terminate. In general, it is best to follow the patient's lead. If the therapy has been at least modestly successful, most patients are agreeable to planning an ending phase. That gives both the patient and the therapist more time to deal with the issues of ending, including reviewing the decision.

Ideally, the ending phase is reached by mutual agreement between the patient and therapist. The therapist may need to emphasize this mutuality. For example:

T: You've had lots of thoughts about ending. What are your thoughts about what my ideas might be?

Often the patient will ask the therapist's opinion. After exploring with the patient her ideas of the pros and the cons, and her fantasies of the therapist's reaction, the therapist could say:

T: I'm sure that you will make a good decision. If it turns out not to be the best thing, you can always return.

If the patient presses the therapist for a definite answer, this is probably an indication of the patient's mixed feelings, which might be explored. The therapist could add:

T: Sometimes patients end therapy with a strong feeling that it's the right time. Others leave with a feeling that it's not quite right. They would like to do further work but they are afraid of what might happen. Or they sense they might get angry if they stayed. Sometimes they return when it feels right.

Occasionally, a patient will feel so conflicted about ending that she will not bring up the subject. If the therapist hears this theme in her material, he might say:

T: You've dreamed of launching a ship, taking care of a newborn baby, and feeling sad in a foreign country far from home. It seems to me that all of these events could symbolize ending therapy. You seem to have been doing well for some time now. What are your thoughts?

Sudden terminations present special problems. Certainly the therapist needs to tell the patient if he feels the patient is acting against her self-interest.

An escalating manic patient suddenly announced he was stopping therapy. He said he needed all of his income, as well as the family savings, for a land investment scheme in Argentina with a broker he had met that afternoon in a bar.

In this situation the therapist advised the patient to postpone any immediate decisions about stopping his sessions or investing his family's savings.

In less dramatic situations, it may be useful for the therapist to review the recent sessions, looking for something that the patient was trying to express or that the therapist was missing.

If a patient declares that she intends to stop immediately, or if she telephones to cancel all future appointments, it is important that the therapist try to arrange a final face-to-face meeting as a "wrap up." This has several advantages. It can help the therapist understand what happened, and he may be able to communicate this to the patient. The patient will feel better because she has ended in a more reasonable and deliberate manner—she will have a better sense of closure. Finally, during the wrap-up session, some of the work of termination can be accomplished.

Even if a therapist has a strong sense that the patient is running away, it is still best to respect the patient's decision to end. The therapist should support the patient's plan because (1) the patient may be right in spite of the therapist's opinion, (2) the therapist needs to help the patient deal with the issues of the ending phase, and (3) the therapist needs to ensure that the patient feels welcome to return at any point in the future.

> Therapist to supervisor: My patient announced that she is going to quit in three weeks. I don't know if I should try to persuade her to stay in therapy or try to help her work through her feelings about ending.
>
> Supervisor: Helping her with her feelings about ending will accomplish both—it's the same thing.

It may be that a minority of therapies progress to a mutually agreeable ending with an optimal period for the termination phase. Many treatments break off prematurely because of issues within the therapy, such as inadequately understood negative transference, or a negative therapeutic reaction (see Chapter 11). In other cases a premature ending may be due to external factors, for example, a patient's economic circumstances might change. Either the patient or the therapist could relocate to another area.

In preliminary discussions about ending, setting an exact date is not immediately necessary. However, when there is a clear decision to end, setting a date reasonably far in advance for the final meeting is important, in that it makes the fact of ending more real.

Most experienced therapists terminate with their patients on a definite date, with the frequency of meetings unchanged until that time. If sessions are only once a week, that procedure is rarely questioned. If a patient and therapist have been meeting two or three times a week, the patient may suggest tapering off gradually to ease the transition. A disadvantage of this plan is that it dilutes the feelings of separation and loss for the patient. There are no hard-and-fast rules, however.

The ideal length of an ending phase depends on how long the patient and therapist have been working together and the nature of their relationship. There are no fixed rules, and Table 16–1 lists only approximations.

The ending phase of therapy is of equal importance to the opening and middle phases. Once this phase has been reached, important new issues and material may emerge. These may be connected with the trauma of leaving, or the patient's unconscious may recognize that a last chance to deal with something is approaching.

Table 16–1
Approximate Optimal Length of the Ending Phase of Therapy

Length of Therapy	Time for Ending
Six months	Several weeks
One year	One to two months
Two years	Two to four months
Three years	Three to six months

The ending phase has two major goals: (1) review and recapitulation, and (2) dealing with the end of the relationship.

REVIEW AND RECAPITULATION

The patient and therapist need to *review* the course of the therapy. They should discuss the problems, gains, and the outcome of the various phases and issues that they have encountered.

Recapitulation implies going back to the beginning. This may occur behaviorally. Symptom recurrences are common during the ending phase. It is as if the patient were saying to the therapist, "See, I'm not ready to leave you. I'm just as bad off as I ever was."

These symptom flare-ups near the end are usually upsetting to patients, who may fear that they have not really progressed after all. The therapist can often reassure the patient by explaining this common phenomenon.

Review and recapitulation in the ending phase can lead to consolidation of the patient's gains as well as to clearer views of what was not accomplished.

DEALING WITH THE END OF THE
RELATIONSHIP—SAYING GOODBYE

The expression of affect is very important in the ending phase. The patient will undoubtedly experience feelings of loss. She may also need to express gratitude or disappointment. As in previous phases, the therapist being with the patient is crucial.

Sometimes a patient will have fantasies or dreams that the therapist will die when she leaves. If termination results from the therapist leaving, the patient may feel that she exhausted or killed the therapist.

Ending therapy echoes previous important separations in a patient's life. As a patient directly experiences her feelings about leaving the therapist, she can further work through issues of loss and independence.

The therapist needs to be open to both positive and negative feelings from the patient. When the patient expresses positive feelings, it helps for the therapist to receive them straightforwardly. Neither grandiosity nor false modesty on the part of the therapist will be helpful. However, the therapist can point out the patient's accomplishment, and that there has been a joint effort.

What has not been accomplished is an equally important subject. The patient needs to express her anger and disappointment. Together, the patient and therapist can mourn the loss of what the patient had hoped for.

An obese woman sought therapy for help in losing weight. After several years of treatment she felt ready to terminate. She had only lost a modest amount of weight, but her relationships with her husband and children were greatly improved. Overall she considered her therapy to have been very succcssful. In her termination phase she expressed pleasure about what she had achieved and gratitude toward the therapist. She also voiced regret about not losing all her extra weight, and disappointment in the therapy and the therapist in this regard.

THE THERAPIST'S REACTION

If the therapy has been meaningful, the therapist will experience sadness at the loss of the relationship with the patient. He may never see her again, and may not even hear what happens to her. He may also feel inadequate about the job he has done, especially if he had misgivings about the timing of the patient's leaving. He may wonder what his ex-patient will say about him. In addition, he may regret the loss of income and worry about filling his hours.

The therapist may also experience warm feelings of having done a good job, as his patient has grown as a result of his efforts.

Depending on his experience and degree of reaction, a supervisory hour for the therapist dealing with ending may prove very helpful.

SHOULD THE THERAPIST BECOME MORE REAL?

When discussing termination, nearly all authors recommend that the therapist share his own feelings of having enjoyed working with the patient, and that he will miss seeing her (assuming these feelings are genuine).

It is also frequently recommended that the therapist become more real as the end of therapy approaches. The advantages of the therapist revealing more of himself is that it may help with the separation. The patient may see him less as a transference object and more on a human scale—someone easier to let go of.

On the other hand, the advantage of the therapist remaining in his role until the very end is the implication that the work of self-understanding goes on, with or without the therapist.

DIFFICULTIES IN THE ENDING PHASE

Difficulties in the ending phase often relate to the painfulness of saying goodbye. The importance of this phase is sometimes not understood:

After a lengthy silence, halfway through the last session, a patient volunteered:

P: There's nothing more to say. Here is your check. Why don't we just stop now?

T: I suppose you're right.

The therapist then ended the session.

This therapist's actions conveyed to the patient that the feelings surrounding saying goodbye were not tolerable for either one of them.

Near the beginning of the final session, a therapist interrupted the patient:

T: Let's not get into anything too deep that we won't be able to finish because we are ending.

This therapist implied to his patient that he believed she was not able to deal with what was inside herself. She was deeply offended by his action, and resolved never to return to him again.

After working with patients in a community clinic for two years, a volunteer therapist was offered a paid position elsewhere in the same city. He informed his patients by telephone that he would not be able to see them anymore.

When confronted by his supervisor, the therapist replied that he was making the change immediately because he needed the money.

This therapist did not seem to realize his importance to his patients, nor the damage caused by his sudden withdrawal.

LEAVING THE DOOR OPEN

It is important for the therapist to leave the door open for the patient to return. This should be done by words and actions. In words, the therapist should tell the patient that she is welcome to return at any time, either for more ongoing sessions, or for just one session if she wishes to talk over something specific. In actions, the therapist indicates the open door by his attitude of respect for the patient's part in the decision to stop.

It may be useful to explore with the patient if she would feel ashamed or humiliated if she were to return after two years.

The therapist may wish to convey his continued interest in the patient:

> T: If you want to, I would be pleased to hear from you in the future about how you are doing. You could call or write.
>
> P: Would you answer if I wrote?
>
> T: Yes I would.

Other issues involving contact between the patient and therapist after termination were discussed in Chapter 10.

It is important for the therapist to tell the patient that the ending process will continue for some time (months or years) after the last meeting. During this period the patient mourns the loss of the therapist. Changes are consolidated and transference feelings may diminish. Over time the patient gradually gains perspective on the entire therapy experience.

CHAPTER 17

Further Learning

- Supervision
- Further training
- Therapy for the therapist
- Psychotherapy as a career

Treating patients under supervision is essential for learning the craft of psychotherapy. The supervisor functions as a teacher, consultant, and advisor for the student therapist. Many experienced therapists attribute their knowledge and skill primarily to the influence of just two or three supervisors.

Ordinarily, a therapist in training meets with a supervisor once a week for an hour and discusses a case in treatment. It is important that the supervision be regular and specifically devoted to ongoing clinical work. Optimally, a student therapist should have a number of cases in treatment and several supervisors. This tends to lessen the anxiety associated with focusing one's entire practice on only one patient.

It is better if the student has both male and female supervisors as well as patients of both sexes. Contact with supervisors of different theoretical backgrounds is also a good idea. When starting to work with a new supervisor, a therapist should reserve judgment of its value until four to six supervisory sessions have been completed.

In structured training programs, supervision is usually provided. Whenever possible, it is to the student's advantage to seek out as much supervision as possible. However, ongoing supervision of a case by more than one supervisor is not recommended, because this can lead to confusion if the supervisors disagree. There is also the possibility of split transference on the part of the therapist in connection with the parallel process, which may add further confusion. This concept may itself seem confusing at this point, and is mentioned here only for completeness.

HOW TO USE SUPERVISION

Therapists and supervisors vary considerably both in their styles and the methods they use. Some supervisors focus primarily on the patient's material and some focus more on the therapist's countertransference (thoughts about the patient and the feelings that are stirred up). Those who focus on the patient's material often want to hear verbatim accounts of what happened in the therapy hour (process notes). Supervisors who focus more on the therapist's countertransference may wish to hear the therapist just talk about the case. According to student ratings, excellent supervisors can be found in both categories.

Beginning therapists are often anxious when they present their work to a supervisor. They fear looking foolish, being criticized, or even attacked. It is important to remember that mistakes are inevitable, and it is the supervisor's job to help the therapist improve. Whenever a supervisor makes a suggestion that helps the therapist's work with the patient, everyone benefits. Hopefully, the supervisor will find things to praise as well as criticize in the therapist's work. Naturally therapists should seek out supervisors with whom they feel safe.

The fact that a supervisor has much more knowledge and experience can make a therapist feel inadequate. The supervisor also has the benefit of being able to reflect on the material, removed from the firing line with the patient. It is not uncommon for experienced therapists to miss simple things.

A psychoanalytic clinical associate (student), who was already a board certified psychiatrist, presented the first hour of his first supervised, psychoanalytic case to his supervisor:

T: The patient came in, looked at her watch, and said that she had been afraid she would be late for her appointment. She added that she was especially worried because her watch did not keep very good time. She wanted to get it fixed, but was afraid to because it was a very old one, something of an antique. She was afraid that the repairman would break it while trying to fix it.

S: (Enthusiastically) Do you hear the transference in that? It's so clear!

T: (Looking blank) No . . .

S: She's afraid that you will harm her instead of fixing her! [The patient was the watch, the analyst the repairman]

Insecurity, perfectionism, or feelings of competition on the part of a therapist can make supervision a painful experience instead of one that is stimulating and rewarding.

It is helpful for the therapist to present the details of what happened in each patient hour as honestly as possible. Sometimes this is not easy. Even experienced therapists are frequently reluctant to present verbatim, clinical transcripts in public. Nevertheless, the more accurate the picture of what went on that is painted for the supervisor, the more the supervisor will be able to understand the clinical encounter and be helpful.

The supervisee should feel free to present his own ideas. He should also feel free to question the supervisor. Supervisors should be willing to explain the reasons for their advice. If the therapist understands the supervisor's reasoning and point of view, he will be more able to make good clinical decisions. Whether or not it is openly acknowledged, final clinical decisions always rest with the therapist, not the supervisor. This is because the therapist is the only person in direct contact with the patient.

THE PARALLEL PROCESS

A therapist had a patient who constantly complained. Nothing the therapist said or did pleased him. When the therapist presented this frustrating situation to his supervisor, he found that nothing the supervisor said was helpful. The first few supervisory hours were unrewarding for both therapist and supervisor.

This is an example of the parallel process: the therapist related to the supervisor in the same way (parallel) that the patient related to the therapist.

In the above example the supervisor was able to point out the similarity of the experience in therapy and in supervision. The therapist understood that he had identified with the patient and was expressing his frustration, *in action*, to the supervisor. As the therapist relaxed and recognized that the supervisor was supportive of his efforts, he began to appreciate the supervisor's advice to resonate with the patient's feelings of frustration, hopelessness, and loss. Not long after that, the patient began to give evidence of bonding with the therapist. Slow but steady progress then followed.

Not all examples of the parallel process are as easy to detect as in this example, but it is always worthwhile to look for its presence, especially in any problematic supervision.

GOING BY THE BOOK

Beginning therapists are both impressionable and rebellious at the same time. On the one hand, they are eager for advice because they often feel lost in their new role. On the other hand, feelings of rebellion arise in reaction to the strangeness of the therapist's role (participating in an intimate conversation without talking about themselves, not answering questions directly at times, keeping rigidly to a time schedule, etc.).

Inexperienced therapists also rebel for unconscious reasons, for example, *because* they feel so needful of direction. In effect they are saying, "See, I'm not helpless. I can figure this out, and you are full of baloney!" Other unconscious reasons include reactions to various painful or frightening contents from their patients' unconscious (and their own).

When in doubt, it is probably better for beginning therapists to follow "the book"—the traditional wisdom and "rules" for therapists. Vincent van Gogh spent years meticulously copying sculpture before he developed his own distinctive style. The modern abstract artist Mark Rothko, whose paintings are mostly blobs of color, was a masterly representational draftsman in his early work. It is only when a therapist has understood the value of traditional techniques, *through her own experience*, that she can safely experiment.

In contrast to the above, it is also true that "throwing away the book" is occasionally helpful. For a sophisticated discussion of this dilemma, see Hoffman (1994).

FURTHER TRAINING

The initial professional degree achieved by a therapist is rarely sufficient. Psychiatrists and psychologists may spend four or five years in residency or graduate school. However, during that time they rarely treat a single patient for as long as two years. Usually, only a handful of patients are seen for more than one year.

Therapists with master's degrees necessarily have very limited long-term therapy experience, due to the usual two-year course of training.

Thus, one reason further training is recommended for all insight therapists is that upon "completing" their training they have had little experience in long-term treatment.

A second reason for more training is to help the therapist continue to improve his skills. Experience is important in the field of psychotherapy, and therapists are able to improve throughout their careers. Ask any therapist if they are not better at what they do now compared with two or five years ago.

Two excellent supervisors gave me contradictory advice about continuing supervision: Dr. A felt that after graduation it was important for a therapist to have a period of practice without supervision, so that he could develop his own style, free of direction. Dr. B felt that because a supervisor had twenty years' more experience than the therapist, he could continually add to the therapist's wisdom. Therefore he saw no reason for any therapist to stop getting supervision. He added that he only stopped supervision when his supervisors died!

Because further training is so important for a therapist, I have found that the initial degree (or discipline) of a therapist bears little relation to his or her competence. So much depends on what he or she has done *after* receiving the degree.

What Sort of Training?

Beyond a psychotherapist's professional degree, further training can be divided into formal and informal training. Formal training might include psychoanalytic training or programs in psychoanalytic psychotherapy given by psychoanalytic institutes or other groups.

The definition of *psychoanalysis* varies somewhat within the field. Ordinarily it refers to a method of psychotherapy conducted four or five times per week for a period of years, utilizing the method of free association, and the concepts of transference and resistance. Usually the patient lies on a couch. Its goal is the formation of a transference neurosis (see Chapter 7) and its resolution by interpretation. Dream interpretation is frequently emphasized. Psychoanalysis attempts to give the patient as deep an understanding of himself as possible.

Not all therapists or analysts feel that this rigid definition is always useful. Freud (1914) considered psychoanalysis to be any therapy that utilized the concepts of transference and resistance. Recently three times per week analysis has been accepted by some training institutes. Some analysts have written that they could distinguish little between their work as psychotherapists and their work as analysts (Weinshel 1992). Jungian analysts consider once a week sessions to meet the criteria for analysis.

Formal training in psychoanalysis is obtained at psychoanalytic institutes. All students (called *candidates* or *clinical associates*) are already licensed therapists with advanced degrees.

Psychoanalytic training consists of three parts: First, the clinical associate is required to undergo a *personal psychoanalysis* with an analyst approved by the institute (a designated *training analyst*). This is usually four or five times per week for a period of years. Second, the student attends weekly seminars for a period of four or five years. Third, the candidate analyzes three *"control" cases*, each under weekly supervision. There is often a paper or examination required before graduation. Some institutes require a graduation thesis and grant a Ph.D.

Psychoanalytic training takes a minimum of five years, and is time-consuming and somewhat expensive (by far the largest expense is paying for one's personal analysis). It also offers professional stimulation, a sense of community, and knowledge that will help a therapist in all the work he does, whether it is psychotherapy or analysis.

It is worth remarking that psychoanalysis is the only discipline that *requires* extensive personal therapy for its practitioners.

A number of psychoanalytic institutes as well as other bodies offer formal training programs in psychoanalytic psychotherapy. Often these are two or three years in length, and consist of classes on theory and technique as well as supervised clinical work.

Informal continuation of a therapist's training can be accomplished in a variety of ways. One of the best of these is to obtain private supervision. In this way a therapist can choose any supervisor he wishes for as long as he wishes. He can sample different opinions, styles, and schools.

The principal problems with this approach for the beginning therapist are anxiety, cost, and overcoming inertia. A therapist should not feel excessively anxious about contacting a potential supervisor. Most accomplished therapists enjoy doing supervision and welcome the opportunity to do it on a private, paid basis.

With regard to the cost, some supervisors will give a reduced rate to younger colleagues. Furthermore, if a relatively new therapist's practice is not full, the increased skill derived from supervision will help in building the practice.

More patients will stay in therapy long enough to benefit, and they will tell others. In this way, supervision can indirectly pay for itself.

Overcoming inertia may have to do with the character of the therapist, or with inner problems that could benefit from therapy.

In addition to obtaining supervision, a therapist can learn from attending conferences, workshops, and lectures. A senior colleague once told me that if by attending a lecture or conference he could learn something that would help even one of his patients, he considered the experience worthwhile.

Reading can also help a therapist learn. One enjoyable method is to form a study group of several therapists with an agenda of reading one agreed-upon article or part of a book before each meeting, which will then be discussed. Other formats are also useful for study groups, including rotating the presentation of cases.

THERAPY FOR THE THERAPIST

"No psychoanalyst [or therapist] goes further than his own complexes and internal resistances permit" (Freud 1910, p. 145).

Although psychoanalysis is the only discipline that requires the therapist to undergo personal psychotherapy as part of training, in my opinion personal psychotherapy is close to an essential requirement for all insight therapists.

Personal therapy for the therapist has several benefits. First, it can reduce therapists' blind spots. These occur when therapists are anxious about unexplored parts of themselves. A therapist who is uncomfortable with his own feelings of depression and loss will have difficulty being with his patients in these areas. If a therapist is uncomfortable with his own anger, he may be overly upset by his patients' anger at him when it occurs, or he may be so "nice" that his patients never become angry with him. Alternatively, he may too readily interpret anger in all of his patients.

A male, Ph.D. psychologist discussed in his supervision a patient who was close to his age and also a master's level therapist. The patient had made good gains in dealing with his characterological passivity for about six months. Then he reached a plateau, where he found he had little to say in his sessions. He then reported the recurrence of a child-hood dream where he was being chased by a monster who arose out of nowhere.

When the supervisor asked the therapist about the patient's competitiveness with him in the transference, the therapist expressed surprise that he had not thought of that himself. The therapist then revealed that he had a retarded, younger brother whom he had always felt guilty about. Thus, he had unwittingly collaborated with the patient in not seeing the patient's competitive feelings in the transference. These were portrayed in the patient's dream, one meaning of which was that the patient felt he was now the monster chasing the therapist. The therapist was able to explore these issues further in his own ther-apy.

A second benefit of therapy for a therapist is that it provides a model experience of therapy from the patient's point of view. For example, being a patient usually heightens a therapist's understanding of how much anxiety a patient experiences in his first visit to a therapist. As the therapy progresses, the therapist has an opportunity to learn first hand from a therapist at work. Consciously and uncon-sciously, a therapist identifies with *his* therapist, and may acquire many of his characteristics.

A behavioral example occurred in a large university department of psychiatry, where a senior therapist used to wear green cardigan sweaters. So many of his therapist-patients copied him that staff conferences looked like a Saint Patrick's Day Parade.

Perhaps the most important benefit of therapy for a therapist is the same as for a non-therapist: growth and the relief of suffering. If a patient (whether or not he is a therapist) is going to succeed in therapy, he must be experiencing a certain amount of pain. As the stresses of their work increase their anxiety, and as they learn more about the potential helpfulness of therapy, therapists in training fre quently seek out therapy for themselves. An additional motive may be to learn about themselves and about therapy.

This discussion should not dissuade a therapist who feels relatively comfortable from seeking therapy to explore its possibilities. Even the recognition of pain or maladaptive patterns may be partly out of awareness. "To get out of prison, first you must realize that you are in prison," runs an old saying. Many therapists in training who sought therapy primarily to improve as therapists have ended up feeling they gained considerably from the experience in other areas of their lives.

CHOOSING A THERAPIST

The choice of a therapist, especially for insight work, is an extremely important one in a person's life. The decision is complicated because there is the possibility of a neurotic choice of a therapist, just as there can be a neurotic choice of a mate. Some people will pay money *not* to have therapy.

How then is one to choose? Unfortunately there are no hard-and-fast rules. Reputation and recommendations are important, but not always right. Talking with the therapist should in some sense feel right to the patient. It is perfectly reasonable to "shop" for a therapist by interviewing several and asking any sort of questions. Obvious signs of disturbance in the therapist should warn a potential patient off. The subtle factor of the fit between patient and therapist is very important, but sometimes difficult to assess.

Sometimes a person has a sense that they would do better with a male or a female, or with a younger or older therapist. A different personality type from oneself is oftentimes a good idea. However, first impressions may convey more about the therapist's social behavior than about how much the patient will eventually benefit.

A young woman chose her therapist on the basis that he seemed very friendly. Later the patient felt that the therapy never got beyond superficialities.

A psychology student chose a former teacher for her therapist because she had felt attracted to him. A nearly unworkable erotized transference rapidly developed.

Conversely, a woman accepted a referral to the head of a local training program. At first he seemed cold and aloof, not at all how she had pictured someone she wanted to work with. Over time, however, she recognized his ability to help her understand herself.

THE VOCATION OF PSYCHOTHERAPY— REWARDS AND HAZARDS

The rewards of a career as a therapist are many. First, there is the opportunity to help people. This is continually rewarding. Though difficult, the craft is an honest one: the therapist does his best to help the patient in return for his fee. In spite of numerous pressures, such as from third-party payers, family members of the patient, and sometimes society as a whole, the therapist remains committed solely to his patient.

Second, the career of psychotherapy offers infinite variety and continual stimulation. Each patient is different and therefore offers a new challenge.

Not everyone finds it interesting to listen to people reveal themselves. What seems like a fascinating unfolding to some may be boring or anxiety provoking to others. Some humans make better airplane pilots, salespersons, chemists, or policemen, than therapists. However, if a therapist is comfortable with the pace of stimulation presented by each patient's attempt to communicate his version of the human condition, then being a therapist will be continually rewarding.

Psychotherapy can never be done perfectly; therefore there is always room for improvement. Being a therapist can be likened to being partly a parent, partly a teacher or a coach, partly a detective, partly a member of a two-man bobsled team, and partly a priest. Doesn't that sound great!

Finally, society still rewards the profession of therapist fairly well.

The drawbacks of a career as a therapist include that psychotherapy is not always well thought of, especially longer-term work. As a popular television commercial used to blare, people demand fast, fast, fast relief! In reality, people make changes slowly; growing up is difficult and requires help from others. These facts make many people uncomfortable.

Potential economic difficulties are another drawback. The future of private medical practice in the United States is uncertain at this time. It seems likely to me that the private practice of psychotherapy will survive, but whether, how much, and to whom medical insurance will contribute for insight psychotherapy is certainly in doubt. Although there are exceptions, public agencies generally do not support long-term psychotherapy. Thus, how busy a new therapist can expect to be, especially over a period of years or decades, is unclear. The only cheering sentiment in this area is that, by and large, the more competent the therapist, the more likely he is to succeed, and each therapist has some control over that.

So-called burnout is another drawback. This sometimes happens when the profession has been chosen too much in the unconscious hope of solving internal difficulties. Over time, if this hope is not fulfilled, a crisis may ensue (Wheelis 1956). Here are two brief examples:

A young man whose parents had both been alcoholics became a psychologist specializing in treating substance abuse. Whenever his patients relapsed, he became angry and depressed. Although he recognized that he had chosen his career symbolically to treat his parents, nevertheless he left the field after several years.

A physician became a psychiatrist after recovering from a depression. Although he became an excellent psychopharmacologist, he never developed the patience or emotional availability to work with patients in psychotherapy.

Finally, various unconscious issues can interfere with professional functioning and satisfaction, such as fear of harming patients or being harmed by them. These are best addressed in psychotherapy.

FINAL RECOMMENDATIONS

I recommend that the beginning therapist try to avoid too much concentration or allegiance to one or another school of psychotherapy (for example, classical psychoanalysis, object relations, Melanie Klein's work, self psychology, or intersubjectivity). This is especially important early in one's career. Because of the field's bewildering complexity, there is a strong temptation to focus primarily on one approach. Attachment to a gifted, charismatic individual is especially likely to create problems. If a teacher is too messianic, the student should suspect a problem.

In spite of one hundred years of work in this field, there is still not even a single specimen hour that is universally agreed upon by all therapists. In a recent study of the psychotherapy of borderline patients (Waldinger 1987), the views of six national experts were surveyed and found to differ from each other on numerous points.

In light of the above, I recommend that therapists of all levels of experience make it a point continually to adopt an attitude of questioning, experimenting, and observing for themselves.

REFERENCES

Bacal, H. A., and Newman, K. M. (1990). *Theories of Object Relations: Bridges to Self Psychology*. New York: Columbia University Press.

Basch, M. F. (1975). Toward a theory that encompasses depression: a revision of existing causal hypotheses in psychoanalysis. In *Depression and Human Existence*, ed. E. J. Anthony and T. Benedek, pp. 385–435. Boston: Little, Brown.

Beck, A. T., Rush, A. J., and Shaw, B. F. (1979). *Cognitive Therapy in Depression*. New York: Guilford.

Bion, W. (1970). *Attention and Interpretation*. New York: Jason Aronson.

Bongar, B. (1991). *The Suicidal Patient: Clinical and Legal Standards of Care*, 2nd ed. Washington, DC: American Psychological Association.

Brenner, C. (1955). *An Elementary Textbook of Psychoanalysis*. New York: International Universities Press.

Ekstein, R. (1983). Personal communication.

Etchegoyen, R. H. (1991). *The Fundamentals of Psychoanalytic Technique*. London: Karnac.

Fordham, F. (1953). *An Introduction to Jung's Psychology*. Baltimore: Penguin.

Freud, A. (1936). *The Ego and Mechanisms of Defense*. New York: International Universities Press.

Freud, S. (1900). The interpretation of dreams. *Standard Edition* 4/5:1–626.

_____ (1905a). Fragment of an analysis of a case of hysteria. *Standard Edition* 7:3–122.

—— (1905b). Jokes and their relation to the unconscious. *Standard Edition* 8:3–238.

—— (1910). The future prospects for psycho-analytic therapy. *Standard Edition* 11:139–151.

—— (1912a). The dynamics of transference. *Standard Edition* 12:97–108.

—— (1912b). Recommendations to physicians practicing psychoanalysis. *Standard Edition* 12:111–120.

—— (1914). On the history of the psychoanalytic movement. *Standard Edition* 14:3–66.

—— (1917). Mourning and melancholia. *Standard Edition* 14:239–258.

—— (1923). The ego and the id. *Standard Edition* 19:3–66.

Friedman, L. (1988). *The Anatomy of Psychotherapy*. Hillside, NJ: Analytic Press.

Greenson, R. R. (1967). *The Technique and Practice of Psychoanalysis,* vol. 1. New York: International Universities Press.

Gutheil, T. G. (1989). Borderline personality disorder, boundary violations, and patient–therapist sex: medicolegal pitfalls. *American Journal of Psychiatry* 146(5):597–602.

Haley, J. (1970). Personal communication.

Hoffman, I. Z. (1994). Dialectical thinking and therapeutic action in the psychoanalytic process. *Psychoanalytic Quarterly* 63:187–218.

Hogan, C. (1995). *Psychosomatics, Psychoanalysis, and Inflammatory Disease of the Colon*. New York: International Universities Press.

Horney, K. (1942). *Self-Analysis.* New York: W. W. Norton.

Johnson, R. (1990). *Transformations of Life* (audiotape). Boulder, CO: Sounds True Recordings.

Kaiser, H. (1962). Emergency. *Psychiatry* 25:97–118.

Kaplan, H., and Sadock, B. (1990). *Pocket Handbook of Clinical Psychiatry.* Baltimore: Williams & Wilkins.

Kernberg, O. (1984). *Severe Personality Disorders: Psychotherapeutic Strategies.* New Haven, CT: Yale University Press.

Klein, M. (1957). *Envy and Gratitude.* London: Tavistock.

Kohut, H. (1977). *The Restoration of the Self.* New York: International Universities Press.

Kotin, J. (1986). The patient-ideal. *Journal of the American Academy of Psychoanalysis* 14:57–68.

Kubie, L. (1971). The destructive potential of humor in psychotherapy. *American Journal of Psychiatry* 127(7):861–866.

Lacan, J. (1993). *The Seminars of Jacques Lacan, Book III: The Psychoses, 1955–1956.* Trans. R. Grigg. New York: Norton.

Langs R. (1977). *The Therapeutic Interaction: A Synthesis.* New York: Jason Aronson.

Lindemann, E. (1944). Symptomatology and management of acute grief. *American Journal of Psychiatry* 101:141–148.

Loewald, H. (1960). On the therapeutic action of psychoanalysis. *International Journal of Psycho-Analysis* 41:15–23.

McGuire, W., ed. (1974). *The Freud/Jung Letters,* trans. R. Mannheim, and R. F. C. Hull. Bollingen Series 94. Princeton, NJ: Princeton University Press.

Meyersburg, H. A., Ablon, S. L., and Kotin, J. (1974). A reverberating psychic mechanism in the depressive processes. *Psychiatry* 37:372–386.

Moore, B. E., and Fine, B. D. (1968). *A Glossary of Psychoanalytic Terms and Concepts.* New York: American Psychoanalytic Association.

Niebuhr, R. (1934). Serenity prayer. In *Bartlett's Familiar Quotations,* ed. J. Kaplan, 16th ed., p. 684. Boston: Little, Brown, 1982.

Polster, E., and Polster, M. (1974). *Gestalt Therapy Integrated: Contours of Theory and Practice.* New York: Random House.

Racker, H. (1968). *Transference and Countertransference.* New York: International Universities Press.

Rako, S., and Mazer, H., eds. (1980). *Semrad: The Heart of a Therapist.* New York: Jason Aronson.

Rockland, L. H. (1989). *Supportive Therapy: A Psychodynamic Approach.* New York: Basic Books.

Sandler, J. (1976). Countertransference and role-responsiveness. *International Review of Psychoanalysis* 3:43–47.

Segal, H. (1972). Address: "A Delusional System as a Defense against a Catastrophic Situation" given at the Los Angeles Psychoanalytic Society and Institute, Los Angeles, CA, January 11.

Sharpe, E. F. (1930). The technique of psychoanalysis. *International Journal of Psycho-Analysis* 11:271.

Solomon, P., and Patch, V. (1971). *Handbook of Psychiatry,* 2nd ed. Los Altos, CA: Lange.

Stolorow, R. D., and Atwood, G. E. (1992). *Contexts of Being: The Intersubjective Foundations of Psychological Life.* Hillsdale, NJ: Analytic Press.

Tierney, L. M., Jr., McPhee, S. J., and Papadakis, M. A. (1994).

Current Medical Diagnosis and Treatment. Norwalk, CT: Appleton and Lange.

Ursano, R., Sonnenberg, S., and Lazar, S. (1991). *Psychodynamic Psychotherapy.* Washington, DC: American Psychiatric Press.

Waldinger, R. J. (1987). Intensive psychodynamic therapy with borderline patients: an overview. *American Journal of Psychiatry* 144(3):267–275.

Weinshel, E. M. (1992). Therapeutic technique in psychoanalysis and psychotherapy. *Journal of the American Psychoanalytic Association* 40(2):327–347.

Weiss, J., Sampson, H., and the Mount Zion Psychotherapy Research Group. (1986). *The Psychoanalytic Process: Theory, Clinical Observation and Empirical Research.* New York: Guilford.

Wheelis, A. (1956). The vocational hazards of psychoanalysis. *International Journal of Psycho-Analysis* 37:171–184.

Whitaker, C. (1969). Personal communication.

Winnicott, D. W. (1965). *The Maturational Processes and the Facilitating Environment.* New York: International Universities Press.

Yalom, I. (1975). *The Theory and Practice of Group Psychotherapy,* 2nd ed. New York: Basic Books.

INDEX